Think Better.
LIVE BETTER.

5 STEPS TO CREATE
THE LIFE YOU DESERVE

FRANCINE HUSS

Published 2014

Printed in the United States of America

ISBN: 978-1-938314-66-7

Library of Congress Control Number: 2014930751

For information, address:

She Writes Press

1563 Solano Ave #546

Berkeley, CA 94707

Interior design by Tabitha Lahr

To my beloved husband, Phil, for forever changing my world in ways that bless me anew each day. My promise to you is to keep creating the lemon-pie dream together.

To the presence and power of Life within me, my partner in something better, from small possibilities to world-changing miracles. I will keep saying yes.

BETTER

LIVE AS THOUGH I HAVE A GREAT PURPOSE. Act with confidence that all of my needs are met. Speak as if my word is powerful. Think from an intelligence that knows all. Create as if the inspiration of Michelangelo impels me. Love everything and everyone unconditionally. Dream with expectation that anything is possible. Give as though I can never deplete my riches. Forgive as though there is nothing to forgive. Breathe as if I have an eternity. Help as if everyone was my sister and brother. Serve as an agent of good. Love without expectation. Consider the earth a living, breathing being. Work with joy to express my talents. Share as though my life depends on it. Look to the future, expecting more good. See every present moment as exactly perfect. Practice peace as if there is no opposite. Receive as though standing beneath a waterfall. Value myself as though I am priceless. Choose compassion in place of judgment. See the brilliance in others. Place every footstep as if a red carpet unrolls beneath it. Expect my desires to be manifested. Hug others as though my embrace heals. Just be me, as though this is my only purpose. Be still and listen as though angels speak to me. Laugh as though my laughter cleanses the air that carries it. Pray as though I am Life talking to myself. Dream joy. Expect good. Speak gratitude. Always choose love.

AUTHOR'S NOTE

ALBERT EINSTEIN SAID THAT IMAGINATION is more important than knowledge, and there are many inspiring stories to confirm this idea. People who realized their dreams, exceeded common expectations, and lived beyond mere averages did so not by living from what they knew or what others knew or what the world knew but by what possibilities they imagined. Mattie Stepanek was a boy who lived only fourteen years because of a rare form of muscular dystrophy. However, in his brief lifetime, he inspired millions with the wisdom and poetry that flowed from his heart—enough to fill seven books. And one of the most renowned American folk artists, Grandma Moses, didn't pick up a paintbrush until after the age of sixty.

You're reading this because you envision something better. It's not that there's anything wrong with your life. The truth is, there's nothing wrong with your life and there's nothing wrong with you. You just want to be happier, more fulfilled, more at peace, more passionate, more . . .

It's human nature to dream, to strive, to desire to live your life your way, and to be your true self. The question is how. Fortunately, the answer lies in your nature and Life's nature. Your decision to partner with Life can yield wonderful results beyond your expectations.

Once you understand that Life is set up to help you experience what you want, you'll be Life's partner and never its victim. You'll find a power that fills you, fuels you, and compels you toward experiencing your true self. You'll be able to direct the same power that holds the stars in the sky and produces an oak from an acorn. You'll be able to use this power to create whatever you desire and dream, including amazing possibilities and even miracles.

No matter what would make your experience of life better, this book can provide a better way of creating it. This book is for you if you:

Struggle with your life and want something better.

Want to achieve your desires with greater ease and less effort.

Yearn for more meaning, flow, and joy in your life so you can make better living possible for others.

Whatever "better" means to you, it not only is possible but can be easier to achieve than you think. Here's how this book provides a perspective on Life and tools for daily living to create whatever you desire:

Part I invites you to be willing to think in new ways.

Part II presents what Life is and how Life works. It provides a basic understanding of your vital relationship to Life and potential partnership with Life.

Part III teaches the Five Step Treatment, a proven tool for aligning your thoughts and mindset to experience what you desire.

Part IV features sample treatments to help you master your thoughts and create your better life.

Caveats

This book is not new-age magic. No candles, incense, or sage were used in the production of this book, nor are they necessary for your use of this book's material. Of course, candles do provide lovely reading ambience.

This book is not religious and will not tell you what to believe (because your personal beliefs are powerful beyond measure). People of any faith, culture, or background will find this material adds richly to their lives and enhances their growth. After reading this book, you may find more treasure in your current church, or you may find more "church" on a mountaintop or as a hidden power you never realized within yourself. This book is about the power of thought and provides a technique for cultivating more creative thoughts.

This book will not change your past, erase damage done, replace therapy, give you better parents/children/siblings/spouses, or excuse the inexcusable. It will not let you off the hook for allowing yourself to keep suffering, indulge in victimhood, or live in stifling, Life-draining ways. I assume you want more than you now experience, and I will show you how to create it.

Note About the Author

Mine is not a rags-to-riches story. I came from a good home, average in some ways and not so average in others. My years in communications and international business were creative, challenging, exciting, and successful by most measures. I achieved success in all of the usual ways, as well as by employing the principles in this book before I even knew about them (although I wish I'd had them then).

Today, I am a licensed spiritual coach with a private practice. I teach classes, serve on boards, consult, and speak professionally. I love the life I am creating, and I am humbled and continually amazed at how these ideas help others achieve their dreams, too. Writing this book about better living is one of my dreams.

My Promise

1. To convince you that you matter. Your very existence is proof of a universe that is creative, expansive, and good. As long as you're being your true self, you cannot fail.

2. To remind you that Life works to support you, and to invite you toward the joy of being your greatest self. You'll be asked to reevaluate—and change—beliefs that are keeping you from your best life.

3. To introduce you to Life's creative process, which you can use for your own benefit. No matter how bad things seem or how good life is, new, invisible possibilities are waiting for you to welcome them into existence.

4. To teach you simple but powerful techniques to harness the nature of Life to create your better life, no matter what you dream. There is limitless potential in thinking better and living better each day.

5. To assure you that whatever you desire, Life conspires to help you achieve. Your dream is an invitation to partner with Life to express your true self. Your dream contains the power and the seeds of its own creation.

Your Dream Is My Dream

I wish you a greater experience of yourself than you ever believed possible. I wish whatever reawakens your true self and makes you feel alive. I wish whatever you wish for yourself, because it blesses everyone (including me). When you live your dream, others become aware of possibilities. You become a shining light for others who yearn for something better. My dream is for everyone to realize and experience what her/his very existence makes possible. One by one, or millions by millions, we'll create a better world.

CONTENTS

Chapter 8: Life Is for You (Because It Needs You)

Chapter 9: New Thoughts for Your New Life

Part I

YOUR BETTER LIFE NOW

[change • improve • dream]

Chapter 1

SOMETHING BETTER

ON A BITTER-COLD JANUARY EVENING, I arrived in Harrisburg, Pennsylvania, for a four-day visit with my mother. She had been officially diagnosed with Alzheimer's disease a couple of years before, but in hindsight, we suspected she had it, and hid it, even longer. The line between ditziness and dementia can be blurry.

As my uncle drove me from the airport to her facility, he found it hard to believe I was actually going to stay with her for several days. He told me he couldn't bear to visit her for even an hour, because she seemed so unlike the sister he remembered and loved. It was unimaginable to him that I would be able to spend that much time with her. "Your mother just isn't who she used to be," he said.

He probably took my hesitation to mean that I was reconsidering my plans, but in fact I was trying to figure out how to say what I needed to say without contradicting his experience with her. After all, we should get to have our own experience without anyone telling us the experience is wrong or that we're wrong in some way for having it.

I believe we create our experiences—yes, the good ones and the unbearable ones. And I believe it's less important to argue about whether we choose our suffering and more important to search the experience for a silver lining that might lead to something other than suffering. The truth is, in every experience there is infinite potential for something to be created from it, and even because of it. Every experience offers the possibility of something better.

What does "better" mean? It means something different to every person. Better is relative to what is. It's often the next step up, according to what you value. When it's beyond what we can reasonably expect or what we can logically explain, it's not just better—it's a miracle.

My work is about helping people use a creative process to create something better. My work exposes me to miracles. So I gave careful thought to my response to my uncle. After all, I hadn't seen my mother in months, and there was no predictable pattern to the progression of her disease. Since Alzheimer's affects each person differently, there was no way to know what I would face on this trip. There was no mark on my calendar for the day that she wouldn't recognize me at all.

"I understand how difficult it is to see your sister with this disease," I said. "Clearly, it's a painful experience. But, with all due respect, I believe there is a light within her that is untouched by this disease—a light that shines as brightly as ever. It's that light I came to see, the part of her that can never be changed." And that's exactly what I experienced.

Did I create that experience? You bet I did—using everything I had learned and everything in this book. Oprah often tells people to take responsibility for the energy they bring into a room. What I brought into my mother's room was a different way of thinking (about her diagnosis) and a different way of seeing (beyond her physical condition). I took responsibility for creating within myself a belief that something better was possible. I took steps to allow a new possibility to happen. And I take credit for having used the creative power of my thoughts.

During my visit at her facility, there was a snowstorm that kept everyone indoors. I couldn't even take my mother for a walk outside. Some of the staff couldn't make it to work, so the usual activities that punctuated the day were canceled. My uncle was probably waiting for my pleas for rescue.

After lunch one day, I guided my mom to sit with me near the windows to watch the snow blanket the garden and the birds gather in the bare trees. I held her hand and tried to get her to recognize these things she so loved, snow and birds. No luck.

However, somewhere in those moments, I became aware of a very powerful, loving connection between us that I hadn't felt in many years. It was the kind of love many feel as a child when it seems nothing in the world exists but your mommy and you. In all these years, there have been other people and other distractions but never as strong a bond as I was feeling at that moment. So many people never get this feeling from a parent, or never again after growing up, or especially once a disease takes claim. I just sat quietly with her and let myself feel this love. In that moment, there was no disease and nothing that separated us in any way. Instead, there was love—only love. This was how I experienced the light I came to find. This was the first of many miracles.

A miracle isn't the suspension of physical laws.
A miracle is evidence of higher law.

For me, miracles are a gift of something greater, deeper, and wiser than I knew before. Miracles are evidence of Life working on my behalf. Like a door that opens to let the light flood in, a miracle beckons us to experience Life in a completely new way.

No matter how you experience your life right now, you can probably imagine something better—everyone can. If you are suffering, "better" is relief from suffering. If you are happy, "better" will make you happier or will include more meaning and fulfillment. If you are having trouble making ends meet, "better" is seeing a way to get all your bills paid. If you are lonely, "better" is feeling loved. If you already have the best of everything, "better" might be the answer to why your stuff doesn't make you feel more alive.

No matter what "better" means to you, imagining it is one of the keys to realizing it. It is your nature to want a good life. It is your nature to want everything in balance and in abundance—health, wealth, love, and happiness. It is Life's nature to help you experience it.

Because you are inseparable from Life's power and possibilities, you can use its creative process for whatever you desire. In truth, Life needs you to bring new forms, creative expression, and experience into the world. Therefore, your desire is Life's desire, too. When you partner with Life, Life works *for you*.

"Life" with a capital "L" is used to refer to that greater something of which you are a part. "Life" with a lowercase "l" refers to how you experience your own life.

This may be a new way of organizing your thoughts: about Life in general, your individual experience of it (your life), and your relationship to it. This book will introduce you to many new ways of thinking, because different thinking will create a different experience. After all, certain ways of thinking (or, more likely, *not* thinking) created your current situation. Changing your situation requires a new way of thinking about it.

Better thinking creates better living.

It doesn't matter if you're down and out or if you want more of the good life you already have. It doesn't matter if you're down to your last dollar or your last million. It doesn't matter if you haven't had a job interview in months or a date in years. Dissatisfaction of any kind feels the same. Hopelessness of any kind feels the same. Being stuck at any level feels the same. The desire for improvement is the same. Fortunately, the way to create something new is also the same. It's possible for everyone. It's possible for you.

Not only is it possible to create something better, it's also easier than you think. In fact, it's about *what* you think. If you can choose a better thought, you can choose a better experience of life. It may sound too good to be true, but it is truly that easy. It's easy because it follows Life's natural and abundant flow. It's easy, even though you live among millions of people who believe otherwise. It's easy, but it requires understanding, effort, and commitment.

"You are today where your thoughts have brought you; you will be tomorrow where your thoughts take you."

—James Allen, *As a Man Thinketh*

Though you dream of a better life, you may hesitate in making a commitment toward creating it. You may be skeptical. Or you may be in so much pain and suffering that you simply can't imagine the life you want. Still, maybe you can be willing—to be willing. Willingness alone can activate a new experience—like prying open a stuck door. An open heart and an open mind become the portals to new possibilities. Be willing to be willing.

If you are already imagining better experiences and better things, you are already in the process of creating them. Your receptivity to a new way of thinking and living is already creating it. Everything begins within you. Indeed, making improvements, living in whatever way is "better" to you—or achieving your dream life—completely *depends* on you.

You are an endless resource of possibilities waiting to be created. Your dream of better possibilities activates a powerful process that creates them.

When you believe it is possible to create something better, something better will be created.

It's About Being Instead of Getting

No doubt you do believe something better is possible, eventually. No doubt you're working very hard to achieve it. Most of us have been taught that we have to *get* everything we need in order to *do* what we want so we can ultimately *be* living the way we really want.

"When I can pay off all my own debt, I'll travel with my grandchildren, and I'll finally feel prosperous." "If I can just earn one more promotion, I'll be able to spend more time at home and finally become a novelist." Doesn't it seem no matter how you try to get everything in place for what you really want, what you really want moves further and further away from you? You're not alone. Many Americans expect to work beyond the typical retirement age of their parents' generation in order to get what they *think* they need to finally be happy. If you're one of them, how about thinking differently?

Try this new thought: Your state of being activates getting. This is true for every form of good, no matter what you desire. Everything in your life gets created according to your state of being. When you focus on the state of being that you ultimately want, everything else will be created to match it. This book will teach you how to achieve the state you want and how to work *with* Life to create what you want.

By focusing on *being*, you start experiencing your life as you want it, starting now, and direct Life to produce everything else accordingly, starting now. You might wonder, *How, exactly, can I start being rich when I can't even pay all my bills right now?* The purpose of this book is to show you how to change your thoughts, as well as your words and your actions, to match what you do want, in order to set a natural creative process into motion to produce it. Can you start imagining what it would be like to pay all your bills in full and have money left over? Can you start using words in your everyday conversation that speak of plenty and abundance, instead of lack and limitation? If being rich would make you feel free and lighthearted, can you think of ways to generate those feelings now, like lying on the grass and watching the clouds drift by?

You create what you think about and focus on. If you think about lack and limitation, you'll create more of it. Instead, focus your whole being on the opposite, and start taking on the life you really want.

No matter what is "better" to you, no matter what you dream, start with the state of being in it now, and all else that follows will correspond to it. Whatever you require to have and to do becomes possible and tangible, because your state of being dictates it.

Entertain the thought of being rather than getting, because Life works with you to give you everything you desire. Your better state of being *includes* getting the things that make you happy and being able to do what suits you. You may not have to wait until retirement to achieve it.

If you ultimately want to feel prosperous, choose that state now. Life's natural creative process will infuse prosperity into every area of your life. It doesn't happen by chance or luck. Life works for you, according to principles that are as reliable as gravity, as unquestionable as the presence of the sun in a cloudy sky, and as simple as $1 + 1 = 2$.

Let me share my own experience. I started my first "business" when I was nine and got my first paying job when I was ten. I didn't need to work, but the work ethic in my family was strong. My years of hard work contributed to groundbreaking research, award-winning advertising campaigns, record-breaking video games, and numerous "firsts" in the corporate world. I helped companies grow and CEOs get rich, and I became an entrepreneur.

Working hard helped me become an expert in creativity and creating success. You could say that working hard worked for me (though we all know that hard work doesn't guarantee success).

Then I discovered a different way, a way of thinking and creating that works *with* Life—a way that always starts with being my true self and always leads to something good. For many years, my focus was doing more and having more. I gained an extraordinary knowledge of how creativity works, and I can turn on a constant flow of creative ideas, for myself or for my clients or audiences.

Shifting my focus to being instead of getting added a rich dimension to my life that was previously missing. Now, when I live first from the qualities I want in my life, I still experience doing and having what I choose, and my life is *more* creative and abundant than ever. The difference is that I live *from* the state I desire, and the doing and having generally fall into place. It feels as though I've shifted from swimming upstream, always fighting against the natural flow, to swimming—no, actually, being carried—downstream. I use the principles and process of how Life works, and Life works *for me*. Now, my idea of a better life is helping you create something better, in a way that doesn't have to be hard and doesn't have to be work.

The Principle of the Thing

Life operates by principles. There are principles of physics, principles of chemistry, and principles of mathematics. We can use physical principles for positive outcomes or disastrous ones. For example, we can use the principle of electricity to provide warmth in our home or to burn the house down.

There are also principles that govern how everything is created. They dictate the way invisible possibilities become visible form and experience. And we can use these principles in many ways, with positive or negative results.

The principles of Life will create what we want—or what we don't want—depending on our use, misuse, or just plain ignorance of them. It doesn't matter whether we are aware of Life's principles or not. We can work against them, creating resistance and making our life more difficult than it has to be. Or we can learn how to use them to our benefit. Many people have experienced the benefits of working *with* Life, and you can, too.

Ageless Wisdom. Modern Results.

The quotes throughout this book will show you many of the diverse thinkers who have discovered and used Life's principles that underlie the creation of everything. No one owns these ideas. Anyone can use them. In your hands rests the decision about how much you are willing to believe, to become, to do, and to receive.

You may discover principles you never knew existed. You may learn things you have observed without realizing their significance or how to apply them. You'll probably become more aware of other people who use these principles to achieve peace of mind, an easy, abundant life, and even great fame and fortune.

You may recognize these principles as simple common sense. That's because their absolute truth naturally resonates with your inner being. You know truth when you hear it. Your heart attunes to it. Your soul sways with it.

You may conceive ways to begin incorporating these new ideas into your daily life and toward your lifelong dreams. That's good, because when you begin using these ideas, your life *will* get better. It is virtually unavoidable.

Better Is a Thought Away

Your thoughts are creative. Everything in your life—everything you touch and every experience you have—began with a thought. Thoughts are individual packets of creative energy, and a belief is a collection of your thoughts.

Thoughts become created in your life as forms and experience—

the ones you like and the ones you don't like. When you replace thoughts and beliefs that are creating what you don't want with ones that correspond to what you do want, something better will be created. The beginning of your better life is only a thought away.

"Change your thinking, change your life."
—Dr. Ernest Holmes, originator of the Science of Mind philosophy

In my experience with my mother's disease, I chose to think differently. The diagnosis of Alzheimer's triggers fear and dread in most people, including me. What will it be like as my loved one deteriorates mentally and physically? How will I handle her own fears of losing her memory and conscious thought process, much less my own? What happens at that moment when, after a lifetime together, I am a complete stranger to her?

I realized that all of these thoughts and fears were based on how this disease was experienced by many others before me. But what if principles were not bound by precedence? What if something else were possible? Here are my choices, which I offer to you to use for any condition or circumstance that you might want to experience in a new way:

- I can choose to allow something beyond average.
- I can choose to look beyond what my physical senses tell me.
- I can be receptive to the infinite potential that exists in everything.
- I can let this experience take me on a new path instead of a dead end.
- I can be open to learning something that transforms me and those around me.

In other words, I can change my thinking *about* this, and thus change my experience *of* this . . . and create a new and better future *because* of this.

The Five Step Treatment

One of the most powerful tools to shift into a new, creative, and more powerful way of thinking is the Five Step Treatment, the focus of Part III.

The Five Step Treatment is based on an affirmative form of prayer developed by Dr. Ernest Holmes, who studied truth common to world religions, philosophies, and ancient traditions. You can learn more about this method and the principles behind it in his flagship book, *The Science of Mind*.

The Five Step Treatment is a technique to change your thoughts to realize that because you are a vital part of Life, Life already offers everything to you. It's a way to shift your thoughts to realize that whatever you require for your highest good and greatest joy corresponds to Life's natural (and powerfully creative) tendency to give it to you. It will help you develop empowered, confident thoughts and beliefs.

It is called a "treatment" because, in the same way you would visit a doctor for a treatment to restore your body's well-being, this is a treatment to restore your mental well-being. It's about realigning thoughts with your true nature, because your true nature and your desires go hand in hand, and they are directly tied to your true happiness and fulfillment.

Treatment is used every day by thousands and thousands of people (who refer to it simply as "treatment"). It helps them consciously direct their own lives instead of being at the whim of others. It conjures peace of mind within any situation. It creates instant access to love, compassion, and understanding. It builds fortress thinking to withstand anything the world puts in their path. It fosters a sense of flowing abundance and possibility, regardless of economic conditions.

Create Your Experiment

Many people have used the principles and tools in this book successfully for years. Nevertheless, you are not reading this book in order to see how someone else has created happiness or prosperity. You want change in your own life.

KEEP A JOURNAL

This book will ask you to suspend old assumptions, examine fundamental beliefs, and change limiting thought patterns. Uncomfortable feelings may arise. A journal will help you process your thoughts and feelings, chronicle the changes in how you look at Life, and affirm what you want to think about Life. You may be pleasantly surprised to see how much change you undertake.

Principles and tools of any kind are meaningless until you see how they work for you and how you can utilize them for your own benefit. You won't truly appreciate the power of these principles until you achieve your own success and start to experience something better. As you put them into practice and apply them toward your dreams, you will be astonished by the results.

Test the principles for yourself. Approach your better life as an experiment. What have you got to lose? The worst that can happen is that you'll continue to experience your life the same way it is right now. And the way it is right now isn't what you'd like, or you wouldn't still be reading this. On the other hand, the best that can happen is beyond anything you can imagine.

To create your experiment, use the Personal Life Inventory exercise that follows. The Personal Life Inventory is designed to provide both measurable and subjective data to see the improvements you'll achieve using the material in this book. It guides you to identify how you're experiencing all the areas of your life right now, and also what you think and believe (and might believe better) about them for the future. There are no right or wrong answers, because it's your personal inventory. The purpose is to identify how *you experience* these areas now so you can evaluate your progress later.

What if you want to change only one area of your life now? Include all areas in your inventory, whether they seem relevant or not. When some things in your life change, other changes generally follow, whether or not that was your intention. Actually, sometimes changing *something* changes *everything*. Once you notice progress in any particular area, you'll be glad you captured this information for every area. This is a really good reason to do the inventory.

Exercise: Personal Life Inventory

Use five pieces of paper and label each one with one of these five main areas of life: health, wealth, love, happiness, livelihood.

Create new pages, labeling each one with any of these other areas that apply to your life: relationships, family, marriage, parenting, creative endeavors.

Assign a satisfaction rating to each area, from 1 to 10 (1 = dissatisfaction; 10 = your dream experience).

Make relevant notes about your experience in each area. Include facts such as employer/boss, bank balance, health data, dating schedule, etc.

Identify three current beliefs for each area. For example: a belief about work might be that work is unpleasant and that's why you get paid to do it.

Write at least one "better" belief for each area. In the example of work, a better belief might be that it is the outlet for one's creative talents and that's why you get paid to do it.

As you apply the information and tools in this book to any (or every) aspect of your life, feel free to go back to your inventory and observe changes in your thoughts and beliefs. Make note of the facts in your life that change, too. See how your new thoughts create new facts.

Personal Life Inventory Tips

1. Define areas of life to track. You don't have to use the labels suggested in the exercise. Create your own. Add as many areas to your inventory as are important to you:

- Confidence
- Leadership
- Sports
- Play
- Family
- Friendship
- Relationships
- Career/Work
- Joy
- Beauty Fulfillment
- Peace
- Health
- Faith
- Social Life

- Abundance
- Connectedness
- Satisfaction
- Creativity

2. Determine measurements of satisfaction and dissatisfaction. In the area of finances, for example, 1 may represent enormous debt, worry, and feelings of inadequacy, while 10 may represent complete sense of freedom from worry about money, a feeling of prosperity, and a sense of capability and responsibility. A 5 for health will mean something different than a 5 for relationships.

3. Make notes. Include notes that create a picture of your current situation and current mindset. In some areas, you might feel as though you are doing okay but experience constant fear and worry that something will go wrong. For instance, maybe you have plenty of money in the bank, but you feel constant stress that it will be depleted by an unexpected emergency. Make any notes that help you capture how this area is manifesting and how you are feeling about it at this point.

Whether you are aware of them or not, you have thoughts and beliefs about all of these areas. What are your beliefs about health, wealth, love, happiness, and livelihood? For example, you might write, "No matter how much money I have, it is never enough," or "I believe I inherited this health problem," or "Everyone else always seems happier than I am, because happiness eludes me." Try to identify at least three current beliefs for each area.

4. Consider "better" beliefs. If you can imagine having a better experience in each area of your life, a better belief corresponds to it. Whether you want to change your experience in all the areas or not, write a better belief about each one anyway. One way to identify a better belief is to first envision yourself in the scenario you want. Imagine having the ideal experience in that area. Ask yourself this question: "What do I think one would believe who has this experience?" Compare the belief that you associate with *having* the ideal to your current belief that is creating a less-than-ideal experience. Notice the difference in these beliefs and commit to changing your belief to a better one.

"Better" is whatever you say it is. If you're experiencing a lot of distress, you may just want to reach a stable state. What's important is what's better for you, whether or not it's a better experience for anyone else. You could also identify an area that's already good but that you'd like to become better than ever. For example, here are some better beliefs about money:

- I feel stability and support that my needs are met.
- Money is no longer an issue in my life.
- Money flows, so I always have plenty.
- I am a money magnet. Everything I touch becomes golden.
- I always have enough money to share with others.

5. Evaluate along the way. Choose when to reevaluate your list and the numbers you have assigned each item. After you have read this book and put the Five Step Treatment to work, you will see the results for yourself. These principles work. They work for everyone, not just for some. They will work for you if you work with them.

It's not uncommon to think better and feel better about a particular area before you see evidence of any improvement in the facts and circumstances of it. Why? Because thought precedes the creation of new form, experience, facts, and conditions. Inner change guarantees outer change. Your better thoughts and feelings are proof that something better *is being created.*

Here is an example in the area of finances. (Money and/or abundance are often used as examples throughout this book, because virtually everyone desires a better experience with money.) Let's suppose you have a lot of debt, your income is not sufficient to pay your bills, and you constantly worry about finances. You will probably assign this area a low number. Once you start practicing the Five Step Treatment, you may notice that you're worrying less and feeling more in control. This new confidence may tempt you to give this area a higher satisfaction rating, yet your debt hasn't changed, your bank balance is the same, and your income is still insufficient. In fact, something extraordinary has changed—you—and outer changes will follow.

6. Pay attention to feelings. Notice shifts in your feelings that indicate change is taking place—*creating something better.* Everything in your life (in this example, either debt or income) is created by your thoughts, and it will be changed by different thoughts. Your decreased worry and increased confidence are the precursors to changes in your debt and income, as long as you stay committed to thinking and believing according to what you want.

7. Keep going. As the numbers inch their way up the scale away from 1 and closer to 10, you'll see measurable results of your commitment. Resist returning to old habits and old ways of thinking at the first signs of improvement. Continue with your experiment. Don't stop short of your goals. Your intention with this book is to create significant improvement and lasting change. Isn't it?

I've done this inventory myself, with amazing results. Of course, like you, I'm still a work in progress, so I continue to fine-tune my beliefs in areas of my life that are important to me.

Chapter 2

WELCOME CHANGE

NO DOUBT YOU ALREADY HAVE IN mind the change that would create something better. However, change doesn't happen in a vacuum. You can't change one part of your life and expect the other parts to stay the same. Every part overlaps with every other part. When you change one thing, everything shifts around to accommodate the change.

There are no limits to the possibilities that are within you and for you. Maybe you've been conditioned to think otherwise and see more limitations than boundless possibilities. However, regardless of the limitation, there has been someone who has overcome it and has proven a different possibility to the rest of us. Someone born into poverty became a billionaire. Someone with physical disabilities became a top athlete. Someone sexually abused became loving, compassionate, and forgiving.

Life works for everyone. What's possible for anyone is possible for you. The power and possibility for change are within you. Once you have a better understanding of your power, you might start thinking of new possibilities.

> "There are two ways you can change your life: (1) Change your conditions; and (2) Change your mind. Sometimes you can change your conditions. Always you can change your mind. Ultimately, mastering your mind yields far more success and reward than rearranging conditions."
>
> —Alan Cohen, author of *Enough Already: The Power of Radical Contentment*

Four Kinds of Change

Change takes several forms. You probably want one of the following kinds of change: 1) to eliminate something you don't like; 2) to transform something from the way it is to the way you hope it can be; 3) to create something entirely new that you haven't experienced before; or 4) to multiply what you already love and appreciate. Let's look at some of the possibilities in these four kinds of change.

1. ELIMINATE THE UNDESIRABLE
- Rid myself of pain, suffering, and health issues.
- Banish worry, doubt, fear, mistrust, indecision, or insecurity.
- Wipe away debt.
- Eliminate financial stagnation.
- Stop addiction to alcohol, drugs, sex, gambling, etc.

TO JOURNAL

Which of these statements matches your current desire for change?

Which of these statements elicit strong negative reactions or discontent?

Identify what appeals to you and what repels you.

If your life is a growing garden, what are the seeds of something new that you'd like to plant and cultivate? What are the weeds of discontent that are keeping your garden from being what you dream?

What kind of change do you want? Relief from what you don't want? Trading for something better? Creating something new? Or more of what's already good?

- Dissolve loneliness, apathy, self-loathing, or unworthiness.
- Remove myself from toxic, codependent, abusive, and/or Life-draining relationships.

2. TRANSFORM INTO SOMETHING BETTER

- Become a better version of myself that I love and others love.
- Feel as if I matter. Believe I make a difference in the world.
- Turn insecurity, indecision, negativity, and pessimism into confidence, positivity, and optimism.
- Turn patterns of victimhood, failure, and drama into patterns of confidence, success, and harmony.

- Make my life more purposeful, creative, and productive, and contribute to the world.
- Turn feelings of loss and lacking into satisfaction, gratitude, and abundance.

3. CREATE SOMETHING NEW

- Achieve a balanced life of health, wealth, love, and happiness.
- Become energized by my life purpose.
- Feel that my life has meaning—that I am connected to something greater than myself.
- Anticipate exciting new possibilities. Feel that possibilities are within my reach.
- Feel that Life is with me and not against me. Live the good life.

4. MULTIPLY WHAT IS GOOD

- Create a career, lifestyle, relationship, and wealth that work for me.
- Achieve greater prosperity to influence change—locally and globally.
- Be more loving, forgiving, giving, and accepting.
- Serve and help others.
- Tap into an endless stream of creativity.
- Experience more ease, balance, harmony, order, and peace.

Changeable vs. Changeless

Change is inevitable, because Life is constantly creative. The basic nature of Life never changes. What Life is and how Life works is made of principles and laws by which form and conditions are created. The principles and laws are changeless; not only are form and condition subject to change, they are in constant flux.

It is *our use* of principles and laws that creates everything, and anything that has been created can be changed. Life doesn't change. But what can change constantly are the *results* of Life's creativity (outer form and conditions). This is the relationship between the changeable and the changeless.

Why is this important for you? The key to creating the life you desire is to work *with* the unalterable nature of Life to set into motion the changeable, creative potential of Life. More simply, you have to know what is changeless (Life's creativity), what's changeable (all form and conditions), and the determining factor between these two, which holds the key to everything you want. *You*—what you choose and how you participate—are the key to what is created.

To achieve your desires, you must start by being willing to allow change. That's often easier said than done.

Fear Creates Resistance

Change often stirs up fear—fear of the unknown or fear of change itself. However, if you want something better, something has to change.

Fear blocks your desires and prevents you from having what you want. It creates resistance that mucks up the process of creating what you want, like throwing a wrench in the works. If it is difficult to release your fear, then, for now, be willing to loosen your grip on it or step around it. If you don't know how to release fear or can't imagine yourself without it, then simply start by being willing—to be willing. Willingness alone can dissolve your resistance and move you in a positive direction.

Be willing to suspend your ideas about what changes will occur for you and what form they'll take. Be willing to let go of fearing the unknown. The unknown is nothing more than the invisible side of Life that has not become visible. The unknown holds infinite possibilities that are for you, not against you. Once you learn about the nature of Life and your true nature (in Part II), you can have a new perspective about change.

Here's how one woman chose new possibilities. Carol wanted to use these principles to help her lose weight, to see if Life could help her create a better experience of her body. But when she explored her beliefs about this, she realized she was afraid that maybe Life intended her to be a fat person. She was afraid if she trusted Life, she might actually get fatter. This fear made only two outcomes possible: staying heavy or getting heavier.

Although it seemed that Carol was working on her weight, she was really facing her lack of trust in Life. And she was experiencing exactly what she feared most: being overweight. However, since everything else she attempted wasn't working, she was willing to try a new way of thinking and create a new life experience.

Carol worked on her beliefs about Life and her relationship with Life. She uncovered (and embraced) a new possibility, which is that Life's nature is to support her in ways that are *for* her greatest happiness. When she learned to work *with* Life, Life worked *for her*. In Carol's case, what used to be a struggle became easier once she was open to change.

The same Life that created you supports you. Life is for you. Life is on your side. It waits upon your word to deliver to you more kinds of good than you have ever experienced. Now *that's* change of a different color, isn't it? When you believe that only good comes your way, you will welcome change instead of avoiding it. For now, be open to the possibility that you can experience your life in this new way.

"Until one is committed, there is hesitancy, the chance to draw back. Concerning all acts of initiative (and creation), there is one elementary truth, the ignorance of which kills countless ideas and splendid plans: that the moment one definitely commits oneself, then Providence moves too. All sorts of things occur to help one that would never otherwise have occurred. A whole stream of events issues from the decision, raising in one's favor all manner of unforeseen incidents and meetings and material assistance, which no man could have dreamed would have come his way. Whatever you can do, or dream you can do, begin it. Boldness has genius, power, and magic in it. Begin it now."

—William Hutchinson Murray (often attributed to Goethe)

Allowing vs. Resisting

Are you willing and available to receive Life's infinite possibilities? Or do your thoughts, beliefs, and fears create resistance and keep your good beyond your reach? A state of resistance prevents the flow of good. A state of allowing cultivates it.

How can you tell the difference between these two states? If it feels bad or it's unappealing, it creates resistance. Doing something you don't want to do creates resistance. Going someplace you don't want to go creates resistance. Anger, resentment, obstinance, mistrust, stubbornness, contrariness, animosity, judgment, blame, spitefulness, and revenge are feelings that create resistance.

Conversely, anything that feels good or appeals to you creates a state of allowing. Allowing creates flow and is marked by a sense of ease. Doing what you love creates the state of allowing. The feelings of allowing include joy, passion, enthusiasm, love, generosity, appreciation, celebration, and attraction.

When you remove resistance, good can flow. As you choose new and better thoughts and beliefs, the shift into a state of allowing corresponds to the manifestation of new and better forms and experiences.

When the state of allowing becomes a habit, your experience doesn't just get better; it gets easier. Challenges will still appear, but if you respond to them from a belief that Life is with you and for you, indeed Life will show up to help you. Empowered beliefs and a habit of nonresistance can smooth, and soothe, whatever arises.

Vision Creates Flow

Either we're pushed to change or we choose change. In other words, either we're pushed by fear (of what we *don't* want) or pulled by vision (of what we *do* want).

When we try to avoid pain or get relief from whatever is causing our suffering, we are motivated by fear. The energy of fear feels like tightness, anxiety, and confusion. We might experience it as resistance when we feel stuck and nothing is changing (even though we may want change).

There's an important difference between putting your attention on what you don't want and how to escape it and putting your attention on what you do want and how to achieve it. Fear has creative energy, like any other thought or feeling. Focusing on what you don't want creates more of it. Become aware that you can choose your thoughts. Realize there's a better use of your attention—focusing on and creating what you do want.

Life's nature is to circulate, to move, and to generate more Life. A body of water becomes stagnant without circulation; our lives can become stagnant, too. We settle into routines, become complacent, and go through every day on automatic pilot. Without growth and forward movement, creativity is hampered. In this state, we might not be suffering, but we're not feeling alive and happy, either.

Sometimes it seems as though nothing is happening, and this is frustrating when you want something new. Quiet moments are necessary for new ideas and new thoughts to percolate and come into your awareness. This state is simply part of a creative process. Even in this period of seeming inactivity, beneath the surface of your awareness, creativity is happening and change is afoot. So, when it seems nothing is happening, you can anticipate that something new and exciting is brewing.

Allowing is conducive to the flow of creativity. It's the ideal state for creating something new. When we are pulled by our dreams, we feel alive, and in this state we are nonresistant. Our dream is like an irresistible invitation.

WHAT IS YOUR DREAM?

Write down everything you dream in your life. Revive old dreams you've abandoned. Invite new ones.

Be playful. Be creative. Have fun. No one else can dream your best life better than you.

The vision of what is possible and what our life might become is inspiring and exciting. Its energy propels us forward. This positive flow feels like being carried in a moving current toward something good. Whatever you want that is better, whatever you dream, it is your personal vision of what can be.

Let yourself feel hopeful for the change you want. Let yourself get excited by the better life you envision. Allow yourself to accept the invitation of what might be. Keep your thoughts focused on what you desire to be, to do, and to have. Stop worrying, running imaginary negative scenarios, and having imaginary arguments. Start dreaming. Create a vision of what can be.

Whatever Life gives you to dream, it guides you to manifest.

Chapter 3

YOUR LIFE . . . UNTIL NOW

Beliefs About Life (in General)

Do you believe in a friendly universe or an unfriendly universe?

Albert Einstein posed this question, and it may be the ultimate indicator of one's life view—and one's life experience. What do you believe? It's important, because *what you believe about Life becomes how you experience your life*. Your answer reveals whether you believe the universe is for you or against you.

In *Excuses Begone*, Dr. Wayne Dyer writes, "When you believe that the universe is friendly, you see friendly people. You look for circumstances to work in your favor. You expect good fortune flowing into your life.

"When you believe in an unfriendly universe, life is unfriendly. You see meanness and spitefulness, greedy ulterior motives, qualities that separate and create hate, frowns and grimaces, bad luck and obstacles."

An unfriendly universe entails judgment, obstacles, competition, blame, shame, regret, suffering, and struggle. It appears that some people are chosen for bounty and others receive the leftovers. In an unfriendly universe, living a good, clean life doesn't guarantee any reward. Luck trumps equality and justice. How can there be a formula for success (or the possibility of a better life) if good isn't equally available to everyone?

On the flip side, a friendly universe is fair and pleasant. When you believe Life is for you and for everyone, what you believe becomes what you experience. You see positive qualities in everything and everyone, beauty everywhere, a stream of opportunities, common good, generosity, and evidence of unseen helpful creativity.

In Part II, you will learn that the universe is innately giving and friendly. The nature of Life supports you and helps you toward your greater good. Cooperating with a friendly universe gets you closer to your dreams, as opposed to what you could accomplish if you were operating in a universe that was unfriendly, unsupportive, punishing, and unjust. Fortunately, you get to choose what to believe.

WHICH IS IT?

Do you live in a friendly universe or an unfriendly universe? What has been your experience? What do you choose now? What does a friendly universe look like to you? Write down your thoughts.

If you are unwilling to accept the possibility of a friendly universe, this book is not for you. This book is not about managing your life in a world that is basically unjust and set against you. It will not teach you to swim upstream, sail a sinking ship, or create your dream with one hand while slaying a dragon with the other. On the other hand, if you are willing to believe in a universe that is friendly, supportive, unconditionally loving, and as reliable as 2 + 2 = 4, you will learn how to partner with Life's inherent power and natural impulse to give you whatever you dream.

Beliefs About Your Life (in Particular)

Your beliefs influence your life. What you believe about Life becomes your experience. Your experience influences your beliefs about yourself. There's an inseparable connection between what you believe about Life (in general) and about yourself (in particular).

Here's an illustration of how beliefs work. A camera captures the image that's in front of it, based on the lens or filter on the camera. A clear lens mirrors the image exactly. Other lenses magnify, widen the view, add brightness, create a more beautiful hue, or turn existing light into glittering stars.

Your beliefs represent a lens through which you see life. Your beliefs form the image in your mind. Your beliefs function as a filter that affects how you perceive the events of your life. You perceive the world according to what you believe.

If you believe the world is unjust, you notice inequality everywhere. If you believe in a fair world, that's what you see. It's as if your mind gathers evidence that proves your belief. Just as you can change a camera lens, you can change your beliefs to change your perception and change your experience.

Is your glass half full or half empty? Similar to Einstein's question about Life in general, this question reveals what you believe about your individual experience of life. It's about whether you believe your life is full or lacking (or something in between). Consider these possible answers:

- My glass is overflowing. It is always full even if I share with others.
- My glass is empty. It's always been empty.
- What glass? I don't have a glass.
- I once had a glass, but someone stole it.
- My glass is broken.
- Do I get only one? I want more glasses!
- My glass used to be full, but now it's all drained.
- No matter what you put in it, my glass leaks.
- My glass is damaged and barely being held together.
- Why are you asking? Do you want to steal it?

JUST FOR FUN

As you consider these possible answers, replace the word "glass" with the word "life." Journal your response to these questions: Do you relate to any of these statements? Do they trigger thoughts or feelings to explore?

Do you know people who are never happy, no matter how much good surrounds them? Where others see fairness, they see inequality. Where there is plenty, they see lack. In the presence of love, they insist on its absence. Their beliefs affect their ability to see and appreciate all the good that exists.

We form most of our beliefs about Life in early childhood. We get our beliefs from others, from our personal experience, or from some combination of both. At an early age, we learn how to work life so that it works for us, at least in ways that make sense to our young, mostly uninformed and unskilled little selves.

Some beliefs are created out of the necessity to succeed (or survive) in our own circumstances. For example, a child living in an abusive home learns that becoming as invisible as possible (physically hiding or emotionally withdrawing) lessens his suffering. Another may simply develop a belief that conceding her own needs to favor others' will guarantee greater reward (such as praise). Each of us forms our own ideas about how to accommodate our fears, get our needs met, minimize suffering, and maximize joy.

It's important to realize when your beliefs aren't benefiting you, have outlasted their initial reason, or are no longer necessary. For example, if you received praise for putting your needs aside for others, you may have become a very thoughtful and kind person. But maybe this belief is the reason you feel like a doormat everyone is stepping on. Or maybe you are still harboring hateful thoughts about an old conflict, even though the fight ended long ago for your opponent. Or maybe you've forgotten what you were fighting for in the first place. Or maybe your abuser isn't even in your life anymore, but you're still carrying out the same pattern of hiding and avoiding attention. Maybe you were taught to squelch your dreams, underperform, or hold back your gifts and talents to appease someone whose approval no longer matters.

If any of these situations touches a chord in you, you can be sure you have a belief about it that's worth changing.

Belief Becomes Experience

Your beliefs become your experience. Conversely, your experience of life reflects your beliefs. To change your life, you must change your thoughts and beliefs—about Life in general and about your life in particular.

Let's look at an example of how circumstances can reveal beliefs that correspond to those circumstances. Once again, we'll use money and finances as the example.

Let's say Carmen is experiencing financial difficulties. Her income does not cover her ever-increasing expenses. No matter how much Carmen intends to reduce her debt, she can't seem to get ahead and actually owes more with each passing year. Unexpected expenses add new burdens. Savings, investments, or retirement funds appear hopelessly out of reach. She might describe her situation this way: "It is a struggle to pay my bills. There is never enough money. No matter how much I try to cut back on expenses, I always come up short. I get my bills paid, but there's nothing left for savings or for the extra things I want. If my income goes up, my bills go up, too, and I never seem to get ahead."

What are Carmen's beliefs about money? Here are some things she might believe: *There is never enough. Money is only for the smart, lucky, and privileged. Sometimes Life goes up, but it always goes down. There is always more need than supply. Good fortune isn't available to everyone.*

What about Carmen's beliefs about herself and her experience with money? Here are some possible beliefs she might have learned or developed: *I'm not good enough (with money). Bad luck finds me. I'm always going to be in debt. Things go wrong for me. Nothing works in my favor. I never get any breaks. I'm not meant to be rich. I'm not worth much. My life's never going to change. Wealth is out of my reach. A better future isn't possible for me.*

Notice that Carmen's beliefs about money go hand in hand with her beliefs about herself and her experience with money. Can you see how any of these beliefs, or a combination of them, might be contributing to her actual experience? Can you see how different beliefs (about something and about ourselves) can feed off each other—in Carmen's case, creating a perfect storm for her struggle? Can you see how Carmen's beliefs distort how she might perceive every situation, not just her experience with money?

It's possible that she *does* get good breaks, things *do* go right, and there *is* potential for more good, but Carmen probably doesn't notice. Her beliefs are a filter through which everything looks dark and dismal. Regardless of how she got these beliefs, can you see how they might be keeping her from a better future? If Carmen were your friend, you'd probably see the connection between her thoughts and her experience.

Are you aware of what you believe about Life (in general) and about your life (in particular)? The truth is, you voice your beliefs all the time. "No one has ever . . . " "Most people . . . " "Most likely . . . " "Usually . . . " These generalizations reflect beliefs. They touch every part of your life—health, relationships, career, finances, family, and so on. They limit your experience now and your expectations for the future.

ASK A FRIEND

You might not be aware of whether you constantly use the words "always" and "never," but others are. Ask a friend or partner about this. Be willing to hear their answers.

Write down any personal assumptions you might be making that you think are being revealed.

Shared Beliefs

What if you can relate to Carmen's hardship but not to her beliefs about it? If you don't share her beliefs, how can you be having her experience? The answer is that some beliefs are so commonly shared by millions of people that they are ingrained in our culture. We may not even be aware that we have these beliefs. And if we were aware and gave them some thought, we might not even agree with them. Without consciously knowing or choosing common beliefs, we pick them up and accept them by default.

Let's be more specific. "Life is hard" is a common belief. It's nearly impossible to escape this belief in some form through the course of the day. You might not think you believe it, but what if the evidence of your life points to the obvious: that it *is* hard? Well, consider that you foster this belief without being aware of it.

Or you simply don't deny the power given to this belief by all those surrounding you who *do* believe in it. Think of how pervasive this belief is in the world, that your life is something to bear, to get through, to survive. Notice how often you hear others say how difficult life is, as if it is a fundamental assumption.

We get many of our beliefs from others (parents, educators, the media, respected leaders, and so on) when we simply accept their ways of thinking without realizing it. We are born into families with beliefs, and it's common to adopt their beliefs as ours without question. Did we stop to consider the beliefs we allowed as our own without giving thought to whether we truly agree with them or not?

"There is never enough" is another common belief that spans cultures and generations. This belief creates poverty, debt, loneliness, unprofessional behavior, and questionable ethics. It fuels sibling rivalry, business competition, and global wars.

"I'm not good enough" is a personal version of "not enough." Once again, it matters little where you may have picked up this belief. What really matters is how this single, overarching belief can affect (and limit) every aspect of your life. This limiting belief makes it impossible to feel satisfied or purposeful or to appreciate your full potential. You might produce riches, a loving partner, and a great career, but if you believe you're "not good enough," you won't feel good about any of these.

"I am not a good enough parent, spouse, child, student, professional, talent, athlete, businessperson." You name it. This belief really says, *I am not good enough at who I am, not good enough just being me.* The truth is, who you are is the key to everything you want. Your true self is a miracle. Life created you to be exactly who you are. Life doesn't need a do-over with you—it may be your thoughts about yourself that need reworking.

BELIEF LIST

Start a list of your beliefs:

1. What I believe about Life (in general).
2. What I believe about my life (in particular).

Set an intention to add more and more beliefs to your list as you read this book. Later, you can itemize beliefs you wish to transform into empowering ones. You can also track the changes in your life that result from changing your beliefs.

Assumptions and Expectations

We tend to expect our life to go as it has always gone. In many cases, expecting more of the same doesn't leave much room for improvement. If you've experienced lots of disappointment, you may have learned not to get your hopes up for something better. After all, if you don't expect much, you won't be disappointed. On the other hand, if life has gone smoothly for you, you likely expect more of the same. Do you know someone who is always cheerfully expecting more good?

In order to experience something new, you must expect something new. How can new possibilities occur if you're not open to them?

Consider moments throughout history in which norms were greatly exceeded, records broken, and seeming miracles took place. In those instances, someone outperformed the average, the historical, the most likely, and the usual. They ignored averages, dismissed trends, and denied generalizations. Instead, they operated by a different set of assumptions. They assumed that what they wanted to achieve was possible. In order for something new to happen, old assumptions took a backseat to a new belief in the possibility of something new.

Nick Vujicic is one person who ignored the "usual" expectations of others and of himself. When Oprah invited him to her stage, the audience was taken aback by what they witnessed. A man without arms or legs boldly moved forward and shattered every assumption in the room.

Nick spoke of breaking through every limitation, mostly in his own thinking, which held him back from living life as fully as anyone else. He told the audience he was happy, successful, and married to the love of his life. He illustrates that nothing is impossible. No matter what conditions we're born into, physical or mental, we can choose how to move forward.

Clearly, Nick is an exceptional example, and some of the others in this book are, too. However, you know someone who has broken through limitations. Someone in your community or workplace has overcome great odds. Go looking, and you'll find enough examples to let you start believing it's not so uncommon. People change averages. You can, too.

Your thoughts and beliefs set the level of your expectations. Celebrate the beliefs that make you receptive to new possibilities. Identify (and change) the beliefs that limit your assumptions. How they came to be isn't as important as your awareness of them and your willingness to change them. The Five Step Treatment and other practices and exercises in this book will help you build a positive belief system that will create new forms and experiences that correspond to it.

Chapter 4

CREATING WHAT YOU DESIRE

YOU CAN USE THE LAWS OF ELECTRICITY to heat a house or burn it down. Likewise, you can use the law of gravity in any way you like, as long as you understand that things tend to fall down, not up. Though these laws were always in effect, it wasn't until we understood them that we were able to *use* them.

If your home is wired properly, you can flip a switch and the lights will work. You didn't create the principle of electricity, and you didn't create the light. But your proper use of the principle makes it possible to flip the light switch and expect illumination.

In the same way, the principles and laws of mathematics guarantee that two plus two will always equal four. The answer corresponds to the equation. Laws are like equations: they follow definite rules for anyone who applies them. As long as you work *with them*, they will work *for you.* When you work *with* Life, Life will work *for* you to create what you want, including your better life.

Part II includes the basic laws and principles behind the creative process by which everything visible is created from invisible energy. This creative process is responsible for the manifestation of everything from the coffee mug on your desk to the job of your dreams.

You can't make two plus two equal five. You can't get rich by thinking about poverty. You can't get well by focusing on your disease. However, there's more than one equation that results in the number five. There's more than one way to use electricity. And there's more than one way you can reach your dream.

You can use Life's laws to create what you want. There are infinite possibilities. What you intend will create new forms and experiences that are as unique as you are. Nevertheless, you must first believe that what you want is possible.

You can achieve only as much as you can believe.

Believe It's Possible

This book will not tell you what to believe. There is no dogma or set of beliefs you must follow. But since your current beliefs are the causative factors in how you have experienced your life up until now, consider whether your beliefs support your highest good.

DREAM BIGGER

Review the dream you wrote in the earlier exercise. Do you know how to reach it? Are you dreaming too small? Feel free to edit your dream and make it bigger.

Be willing to create and cultivate beliefs that are devoted to what you want. Above all, be willing to believe *in* what you want. No matter what you dream, be willing to believe it is possible.

This isn't about pie-in-the-sky dreaming. Possibilities are part of Life. Possibilities are the rich, fertile field from which everything sprouts, blossoms, and grows. Possibilities are the infinite, invisible energy that becomes real form and experience.

Think about this: Every visible form that exists right now was created from invisible possibilities. Your smartphone originated in someone's mind as an idea, a thought that corresponded to a possibility, a mental prototype that became the actual thing. The mighty oak began as an acorn; before it was an acorn, it was invisible potential energy.

Scientists long ago discovered the infinite potential of invisible energy. The creative process that turns invisible energy into a visible form and an idea into a smartphone can turn your invisible dream into a real experience. Right this minute, every good thing you can imagine is already a possibility, waiting to be made real. Your dream may be only a possibility, but your belief in it is a necessary part of the process that will create it.

For now, be willing to believe in possibilities. Be willing to change what you believe about Life and what your life can become.

For now, choose the changes you want. Dream your dreams. Suspend any negative or unproductive beliefs you have about your dream, its probability of happening, the means to make it real, or the fears that keep you from dreaming it. How much you are willing to believe will greatly determine the experience you will have in creating it. For now, allow yourself to dream, and believe your dream is possible.

> "If you know how to reach your dream, you're not dreaming big enough."
> —Deborah Johnson, founder of Inner Light Ministries and The Motivational Institute

You Deserve What You Desire

The widely held belief of "not good enough" runs through many people's life stories. If it's part of your story, it will keep you from believing in yourself and in your dream. More specifically, it will keep you from experiencing your true self and the dream you deserve. The source of that belief isn't as important as your willingness to release it—permanently.

Your story is a combination of the facts of your life and your perceptions of the facts. Have you ever compared an old family story with another member of your family and realized you both have different versions of the same story? Your story is your version of your life. It includes your beliefs about Life and your beliefs about yourself.

What do you do when the belief of "not enough" (or any other limiting belief) is part of your story? What if there is a lot of evidence in your past (no matter how juicy, dramatic, painful, or shameful) that supports your "not enough" belief? Well, you can choose a new story. You can rewrite your story. Find evidence that proves you *are enough*, and write a new story from those facts. Which do you choose—your old story or your new future?

If you've spent your lifetime believing you are not enough, you probably feel unworthy, have low self-esteem, or both. Years of believing you're "not enough" to achieve what you want often creates a corresponding belief that you "don't deserve" what you want. Unfor-

tunately, no matter how much you desire, you'll never reach fulfillment until you believe you deserve what you desire.

WHAT DO YOU DESERVE?

Journal your feelings about worthiness. Does this
make you feel good or bad? Can you identify
a time when you felt you deserved what you
wanted? Write how that made you feel. Are you
willing to feel this now? Can you multiply this
feeling within you?

Did you know that many lottery winners eventually end up right
where they started financially? The lottery may have made them instantly rich, but if they don't believe they are rich, the experience of
wealth cannot last. Experience follows belief. If they did not believe
they deserved millions of dollars or did not believe that they were
fundamentally good enough to steward great wealth, their experience of life (and their money) would correspond to their beliefs—
namely, not enough.

In the next section of this book, you will learn the nature of Life
and your relationship to it. You will discover that your very existence
proves your matchless, unquestionable, immeasurable worth.

Life's expressive and creative nature requires you to fulfill its nature to express and create.

You are a piece of the puzzle that makes Life complete.

You are necessary to Life. You matter.
You make a difference.

Life withholds nothing from you. It gives you as much breath as you can breathe—the end of one breath is the beginning of the next. Life gives you as much love as you can give—give it all away, and there's always more. Life gives from an infinite supply.

Your worthiness is not in question. Somehow, you may have accepted a question of your worthiness. Whether someone told you that you were not valuable or you simply (mistakenly) deduced this yourself, if a feeling of unworthiness has found its home in you, it will stay there until you demand that it leave. When you realize that your very nature makes it impossible for you to be unworthy of anything, the feeling of unworthiness will no longer be able to keep you from every good thing you can imagine.

How Much Can You Receive?

My dear friend Rev. Dr. Lloyd George Tupper tells a story of a pivotal moment when he realized the importance of being willing to receive. It was in Phoenix, Arizona, when Lloyd attended classes in the study of the science of mind and philosophy.

"In the first night of class, my teacher said he wanted to begin the class by having everybody agree on one principle put forth in biblical scripture. Naturally, we were all very attentive and listened closely. He said, 'I would like us all to agree that it is God's good pleasure to give you the kingdom.' There was a lot of murmuring and grumbling, and I noticed that most of it was coming from me.

"What my teacher said (and what I had already read before) seemed entirely too good to be true.

"So, he started asking us to raise our hand if we had a question. I'd put my hand up and simultaneously pray to God he wouldn't call on me, and then I'd pull it down. I'd put it up, and I'd pull it down.

Finally, he said, 'Yes, Lloyd?' I answered, 'I'm having a hard time accepting what you're saying. It's just too good to be true. I've just gone through a hellish experience in my life. My faith has seemingly failed me. I've lost all my worldly possessions.' I went through the whole woe-is-me diatribe.

"Finally the teacher said, 'Lloyd, this is going to be your first assignment, and this is going to be a tough one for you. I want you to entertain this idea: If indeed it is God's good pleasure to give you the kingdom, can you develop the graciousness to receive it?'"

HOW MUCH CAN YOU RECEIVE?

To Life, there is no difference between creating a little and creating a lot.

Review your answers to the Choose Your Change exercise. Identify how much good feels good, versus how much good begins to feel uncomfortable.

Are you willing to receive as much as you desire?

"This changed my life. It was like I was being asked to develop good manners. Maybe I should stop putting my elbows on the banquet table of life in God's presence and start receiving what is being offered. I decided that if it is God's good pleasure to give me the kingdom, I am going to show up to get it. And that was the way it started for me.

"Now, it's second nature to me. I absolutely believe if I can conceive it, God can deliver it. It's a question of what level of faith am I going to raise myself up to, to get the goods."

Consider the possibility that whatever seems too good to be true might actually be true—no matter how good it seems.

If you are willing to believe you are a necessary part of Life's operation, then be equally willing to receive the bounty that goes along with it. Imagine a red carpet unrolling beneath your footsteps. Are you willing to receive graciously wherever the red carpet takes you, no matter how good it seems?

You Matter. Your Dream Matters.

You matter. Many find this idea hard to believe, but the reason you matter is so simple, it takes only four statements to explain it:

You exist. Therefore, there must be some reason for you, some purpose. Your existence points to your purpose, and your purpose must be tied to your existence.

You're here because Life requires you to create and express what is possible only by you. Life needs you as a piece of the whole puzzle that cannot be filled by anyone else. Therefore, what makes you special makes you important. Whatever fulfills you ultimately matters to the whole of Life. Being happy, prosperous, creative, healthy, joyful—living your dream—is what Life desires for you.

Being your true self and living your way matters. This is your only true purpose.

You'll be happy when you express your true nature. Life will help you bring forth new possibilities that match your nature, because Life requires your participation in creating them. In other words, Life will supply everything you require to be your true, happy self.

"The privilege of a lifetime is being who you are."
—Joseph Campbell, *Reflections on the Art of Living*

What does this mean, "your true self"? It is your self beyond your facts, your story, your family, and your circumstances. It is your self that is not limited by your age, your education, your size, shape, or sexual orientation. It's being who you really are.

It's what makes you special and unlike anyone else. It's your unique combination of gifts and talents that have never been duplicated and never will be. It is your self that feels alive, creative, free, and joyful when you're expressing what's uniquely you. It is your self that is perfect exactly as you are. It is your true nature as a microcosm of Life's nature.

Gifts and talents don't refer to any particular skill or ability. It's what you love and what makes you feel alive. There are no criteria or rules, because each person is unique. There's no quality or gift that is more or less valuable. People who are true leaders feel energized by leading. People who love to help others are excited by opportunities to feel needed and useful.

Since everyone is vital, there is a perfect place for everyone. In other words, for every way there is to express Life, there is someone whose unique makeup and idea of fulfillment match that expression. Fortunately, we all have different and unique gifts and dreams.

Maybe you know your true nature. Or maybe you're too busy being a mom, a family provider, a caregiver, a coach, a petty-cash distributor, a chauffeur, and a cook to be aware of what's true. If any (or all) of these roles give you joy unbounded, you're living your true life. If they don't fulfill you, it's time to find what does.

What makes you feel alive? What kinds of expressions and ways of being make you happy? What gives you deep satisfaction? What feeds your soul? What makes you purr with contentment? Here are some possibilities of being:

Artistic.	Visionary.	Gregarious.
Creative.	Motivating.	Dedicated.
Rhythmic.	Inspiring.	Devoted.
Balanced.	Patient.	Committed.
Harmonious.	Considerate.	Sweet.
Orderly.	Optimistic.	Kind.
Organized.	Social.	Loyal.
Generous.	Understanding.	Expansive.
Healing.	Communicator.	Enthusiastic.
Helping.	Insightful.	Refreshing.
Caring.	Calm.	Determined.
Compassionate.	Grounded.	Positive.
Accepting.	Methodical.	Spontaneous.
Graceful.	Fair.	Logical.
Loving.	Playful.	Thoughtful.
Nurturing.	Childlike.	Luminous.
Leader.	Serious.	Carefree.

You don't have to stop being a mother or a caregiver in order to express who you truly are. Expressing your true nature will lead to more happiness *within* your life. When you bring more of yourself into each role and situation, you'll experience it differently. Shine your specialness into your circumstances, and they'll light up. Make

YOUR TRUE SELF

Does all this talk about being your true self stir memories? Moments of joy and satisfaction? What words describe you? What makes you feel vitally connected to Life?

Journal your thoughts, feelings, memories, and insights. Rediscover your true self.

Write your true self a letter. What do you want to say to it?

a decision to contribute whatever it is that makes you feel alive. Being (who you really are) precedes having (what you really want).

Being Leads to Doing and Having

When you start living according to your nature, it's as if Life opens doors of possibilities that have your name on them. Being your true self leads to possibilities of doing what you love and having everything that makes you happy. Your essential nature provides the equation that results in your dream. What makes your heart sing? What ignites your zest for life? What touches your essential nature? Here are some possibilities:

- Change or create a career. Improve my current job. Leave my current job.
- Travel far and wide. Make time to visit a nearby city.
- Undertake more adventure. Make my life a bit less of an adventure.
- Start a sport. Return to a sport. Change sports.

- Start my own business. Sell my business. Expand my business.
- Start a family. Improve my family relationships.
- Learn a new skill. Study a new subject. Become an expert.
- Pursue an art form. Learn a hobby or craft.
- Spend more time in nature. Plant a garden. Weed the garden.
- Spend more time with my family.
- Buy a new home. Sell my home.
- Rent a new apartment. Find a new roommate.
- Get organized. Clean the garage. Organize closets.
- Find a loving partner. Improve a relationship. End a relationship.
- Become financially free and stable. Make more money. Eliminate debt. Reduce debt. Get help with debt.
- Treat my body as a temple. Accept my body. Love my body.
- Change my exercise routine. Begin an exercise routine. Move more.
- Be perfectly healthy. See health as a possibility.
- Heal a health challenge. Experience health in new ways.
- Love my relatives. Accept my relatives. Forgive my relatives.
- Love myself. Accept myself. Forgive myself.
- Love everyone. Accept everyone.
- Have more fun. Have more balance in my life. Make time for fun.

YOUR BETTER LIFE

What do you really want? Take a look at these examples, or create your own. What does better living mean to you? Keep working on your dream.

Being yourself will lead to your fulfillment. Appreciating and loving your true self will bring contentment. Everything flows *from* your personal way of expressing Life. Your choice of *being yourself* leads to the creation of doing and having whatever corresponds to it. Your state of being will lead you to doing and having what will make you happy.

Life will create everything around you to match what you give and what you love. The world will shift to accommodate this new you, the true you. If you're inquisitive, opportunities and situations will arise that require your curiosity and allow your gift to flourish. If you're a natural-born healer, Life will connect you with those who need healing.

The world needs healers, problem solvers, dancers, visionaries, leaders . . . you name it. The world needs you to be exactly who you are, to live your best life, and to experience your dream.

> "I say follow your bliss and don't be afraid, and doors will open where you didn't know they were going to be. If you follow your bliss, doors will open for you that wouldn't have opened for anyone else."
>
> —Joseph Campbell, *The Power of Myth*

Summary of Part I

You create your experience of life. Thoughts and beliefs are creative. You can change your life—and create your better life, your dream life—by changing how you think and what you believe.

Life works for you when you work with Life. Life works according to laws and principles that you can use to create what you want.

What you believe about Life is how you experience Life. What you believe about yourself is what you create for yourself. What you believe you deserve is what you get. What you believe is possible becomes possible.

Change expectations from what has been to what can be. Create something new by shifting patterns of thinking. Believe in something new and expect something new.

Resistance (fear, limiting thought, disempowering belief, negative emotion) blocks the good you desire. Allowing (better thoughts, empowered beliefs, welcoming change, positive emotions, your true nature) cultivates the flow of good.

Being your true self is your purpose and your key to happiness. Being yourself leads to doing and having everything you want. What makes you special makes you vital to Life, which will provide all you need to express your true nature.

What's Next?

If Part I inspired you with possibilities for creating something better, Part II will explain how it's possible. A brief explanation of what Life is and how Life works is enough to set you on the path to work with Life (not against it) in creating what you want. You'll learn the creative process by which everything becomes manifested, and you'll learn about the role of your thoughts and beliefs in that process.

Part II

LIFE'S NATURE IS
YOUR NATURE

[presence • power • principle • law]

Chapter 5

THE NATURE OF LIFE

Life, That Greater, All-Encompassing Everything

Once you realize how Life works, you can work with Life to create your better life. Once you realize Life's power is your power, you can direct it. Once you realize your relationship to Life, you will see that Life already offers everything you require to live your best life, your way. So, it's worth your while to examine this thing called Life.

Every part of Life contains the whole of Life. Yet the whole is always greater than any part.

Biology is the study of natural, organic Life. Paleontology is the study of the origins of Life forms. Astronomy is the study of the cosmos. Sociology. Psychology. Theology. Kinesiology. Physiology.

Dermatology. Etymology. Genealogy. Hematology. Ichthyology. Gemology. Mythology. Radiology. Musicology. Audiology. Neurology. Ophthalmology. Meteorology.

Each of these fields represents the quest to understand how Life works and how Life is expressed within a certain context. The ultimate purpose of each of these disciplines is to apply its understanding in a way that improves, enhances, and furthers the expression of Life in general and our human experience of life in particular.

Meteorologists, for instance, study weather patterns to help forecast and prepare for the impact of weather. Their work has led to the development of early-warning systems that save lives in the path of hurricanes, tornadoes, and other major weather systems.

Sociologists study the many ways in which people behave and relate to one another in relationships, in organizations, in various environments, and in cultures. Their purpose is to optimize how people live and work together.

Study yields discovery. So what should we study in order to discover how to partner *with* Life? Study all of it, not just one particular aspect of it. In the next few pages, we'll study Life from the broadest vantage point in order to understand its nature across all boundaries. The greater, all-encompassing definition of "Life" holds truths that exist in every particular part of it. These universal aspects of Life apply to biology and psychology and every other -ology. The universal nature of Life is what you need to know about in order to discover that Life's nature is your nature, too.

What's In a Name?

If we assume "Life" consists only of what we currently understand, we limit its definition to our current understanding. Surely there is more to Life than what we understand or have discovered (otherwise, there would be no further purpose to scientific study).

We could refer to Life as "Mother Nature," but this excludes everything that is not of nature, such as anything created by humankind. Similarly, defining Life as "the universe" ignores the uncharted galaxies beyond our human awareness or anything other than the three dimensions (length, width, and depth) of human experience. (In fact, scientists working on string theory have identified ten dimensions.)

In order to glean universal laws and principles that apply to all of Life (including what we know and what we have yet to discover), we will consider Life in the supreme context—omnipresence.

Om•ni•pre•sent, adj.
The quality of being everywhere at the same time.

Omnipresence means Life is present everywhere and absent nowhere. It's been a focus of study throughout every age of humanity. It has too many names to list, but here are a few: Ra. Elohim. Yahweh. Allah. God. The universe. Energy. Spirit. All in All.

Sadly, so much has been taught, told, and twisted in the name of God that the name has lost its meaning for many of us. It is used to promote love and hate, peace and war, inclusion and separation. How much of what we have been exposed to was born of a kind of ignorance (at best) or from wicked intentions (at worst)? It's no wonder that the name God provokes a broad range of reaction. Many of us tune it out as soon as we hear it.

In some cases, our own experience influences our idea of God. I was ten years old when my father died. My mother tried to calm my confusion by telling me that God must have needed him. To her, it was the most loving explanation, but to me, she gave me a target for blame and responsibility. A twisted idea of God formed within me for many years; I may never fully realize its impact. Not being on speaking terms with the All in All surely creates its own limitations.

Unfortunately, when we cut ourselves off from everything about God, we also miss *anything* about God. We eliminate the things that we might actually want to hear and understand, especially that which might be useful and inspiring in our own life. Keeping ourselves at a distance from everything that is God-related is like throwing the baby out with the bathwater.

Consider suspending what you have been conditioned to think up until this point. For now, try replacing "God" with "the God of *my* understanding." Or, if you prefer another title, such as Life or Spirit, consider using "Life as I understand it." This puts aside the assumption that there is only one right way to understand God, or Life, or Spirit.

LIFE

Scientists study its mystery. Theologians study its meaning. The word Life is used throughout this book as something everyone can agree on.

Be willing to look at Life in a new and different way. Consider creating a brand-new understanding of Life that *suits you and is personal to you*. Life *is* personal to you because you are an expression of Life. You are not separate from Life. Therefore, consider a new definition of Life that feels good, supportive, and inspiring and is as original as you are.

Nothing has had a greater impact on my life than creating my own new understanding of Life. When I thought I was doing everything myself, I accomplished much. But when I became willing to partner with Life, everything became better than I had ever imagined. For example, opportunities present themselves to me that match my intentions and goals. The perfect people show up in my life and help support and further my dream. Every day, there are new ways in which Life works for me because I changed how I think about Life.

It doesn't matter what you call Life, because nothing changes its nature, and nothing excludes anything from it. Omnipresent Life includes everything, into infinity. Since everything is included in it, its nature is universal, and therefore, everything shares its nature. Let's agree on this as the context in which to view Life and as our starting point in seeing Life in a new way.

Once you see Life differently, you can experience life differently.

Once again, all you need to do is to be willing, or to be willing to be willing. Assuming your willingness, let us proceed to consider the nature of Life by starting with a clean slate.

There is more to Life than we see or experience.

Life Is as Life Works

What Life Is describes universal properties or qualities of Life in the visible as well as the invisible. These are the principles of Life, unchangeable truths that apply to every aspect of Life and to all conditions. Whether you are looking at a butterfly or a rock, Life's principles are present in them, in you as the observer of them, and in everything in between.

> **Prin•ci•ple, n.**
> Truth of Life. A fundamental, primary, or general law or truth that is unalterable by any other truth or fact.
>
> **Law, v.**
> Action of Life. Describes an action or a system of operation that occurs by its own power. Laws are unalterable; there are infinite applications of laws.

How Life Works describes the action by which Life operates and the laws that govern every aspect of Life. Similar to laws of the physical world (the laws of electricity, the laws of gravity, etc.), the universal laws of Life are in constant operation, whether we are aware of them, whether we understand them, or whether we make it our business to use them to our benefit.

CONSIDER THIS

By understanding what Life is and how Life works, you can work with Life to let Life work for you. You can work with Life to be, do, and have whatever suits you.

Life works with you and for you to experience your greatest joy and fulfillment. Life is your partner. Your fulfillment is also Life's fulfillment.

Chapter 6

WHAT LIFE IS

Life Is More Than You See

Take a look at something in the distance: a mountain, a cloud, or a skyscraper. Between you and what you are observing is nothing but air, though any scientist will tell you there is enormous energy in the nothingness of air. There is more energy in what you *don't* see than in what you *do* see, because all the form you see is merely energy that has slowed to a rate of vibration that gives it form. However, there is still energy that has yet to become form, and this energy is as real as any form but is not limited by form.

There is more that is invisible than is visible. This very important scientific fact has great implications for you, because the invisible holds the possibilities for the life you desire. Later in this book, you will learn how to bring your possibilities into visibility, but for now, understand that Life is more than what you observe.

Here is a simple exercise that illustrates the point that Life is more than what your physical senses perceive. Look at a candle or a

CONSIDER THIS

Right where you are now, there is more than you can see. More between you and whatever your eyes are set upon. More activity, more power, and more invisible substance that has yet to become apparent to you in the way you are seeing.

Between you and what you are looking at are potential, possibilities, and power. Your physical senses can perceive only the physical world. There is much more than just the form that is apparent to your senses.

If you can accept that there is more to see than what appears, then you can begin to accept that there is more that is. When you accept the possibility that there is more that is, then you can begin to assume more and expect more and ultimately experience more.

single bright light. Focus on it and allow nothing else in your sight. Allow your eyes to relax and your focus to soften. Soon, you will begin to see not one flame or light, but two flames, maybe even three or four. Stay in this relaxed mode, and maintain the multiple images for a few moments, so that you can really sense that you are seeing more than one image.

With your very own eyes, did you not just see something that is not there in physical form? Without any physical instrument and without adjusting the physical position of your body, you saw something different than you originally did. Correct?

This simple optical illusion illustrates how you can see something one way that is obvious and indisputable to your physical senses, yet you can also perceive the same thing in a different way. Moreover, you can allow yourself to see something else in the same place.

When you change focus, a new sight emerges. You could say a new possibility emerges—the possibility of more than what you saw before.

Relying solely on what you perceive in visible form leaves out all that is invisible, which, you will soon find out, is, well, practically everything.

How much of Life is there? Infinite.

What does Life include? Everything.

Where is Life absent? Nowhere.

Life is Everywhere

Life's omnipresence means there is no place where Life does not exist, no place where Life is absent, and nothing that is without Life. There is only Life and nothing other than Life.

Nothing can oppose Life. Therefore, everything is included in Life and shares the qualities of Life.

Life is fully present everywhere and is not more or less present anywhere. Life is as present in a weed as it is in a rose. Life is as present in a rock as it is in a sunset. Life is as present in disease as it is in health. Life is as present in a liar as it is in a saint.

Life does not treat anyone differently from anyone else. It might look like someone got more than his or her fair share and someone else got less, but looks are deceiving. Everyone is invited to the same bountiful buffet. Everyone has access to it, but you can't enjoy it if you're not aware of it or don't show up for it.

You have the ability to *feel* separate from Life and to *block* its infinite potential. Conversely, you can maximize your experience of life by cultivating a feeling of connection with its power and its potential. You can capitalize on your inseparable unity with Life and all that

Life is. You can claim your buffet ticket and indulge. The profound implication of Life's omnipresence—One Life—means that Life is in you. In other words, wherever you are, Life is.

CONSIDER THIS

No matter what your experience of life, Life has never been absent for you, or for anyone else. Life has never deserted you, and it never will, because it cannot. Life and all of its qualities are within you. You are as immersed in Life as a drop of water is immersed in the ocean.

It is impossible for you to be separate from Life and all of its qualities. It is impossible for you to escape Life. It is impossible for you to be separate from its infinite potential.

There is only One Life.
***All* of Life is where *you* are.**

Life Is Infinite

No matter how many galaxies scientists have identified, there are infinitely more to be found. Life has no limits whatsoever, not even a beginning or an end. It is infinite.

Every quality of Life is infinite. Life is infinitely intelligent.

In•fi•nite, adj.
Unlimited or unmeasurable in extent of space, duration of time, etc. Unbounded or unlimited; boundless; endless.

Life is infinitely creative. Life is infinitely abundant. It is virtually impossible for our human brains to understand and conceive of the infinite. Our human brains can go only so far, because we create boundaries of the infinite based on our experience, perspective, and imagination. In other words, our own limited experience and perspective make it impossible to perceive infinity.

> **"Imagine the vastest capacity you will, and having filled it with the infinite, what remains of the infinite is just as infinite as before."**
> —**Thomas Troward,** *The Edinburgh Lectures*

In imagining the infinite, we tend to think only a little further than what we already know or have experienced. Here is an illustration. Imagine being alive several hundred years ago. In the fifteenth century, the printing press and vodka—which some consider great contributions to human civilization—were invented. If you were living at that time, would you be able to imagine what could be next on the horizon?

In the sixteenth century, it was discovered that the earth revolves around the sun, and not vice versa. Amazing, yes, but to others, nothing compared with the life-changing inventions of the flush toilet and the pencil. Given those luxuries, what else could anyone dream up?

In the nineteenth century you would have found yourself made so dizzy by inventions that you might have assumed there was nothing new left. Lightbulb. Telephone. Typewriter. Sewing machine. Assembly line. Battery. Tin can. Steam locomotive. Stethoscope. Soda fountain. Electromagnet. Matches. Reaper. Steamboat. Bicycle.

Monorail. Lighter. Fountain pen. Cement. Saxophone. Refrigerator. Safety pin. Condensed milk. Linoleum. Dynamite. Vacuum cleaner. Levi's jeans. Stapler. Cash register. Safety razor. Roller coaster. Automobile. Dishwasher. Ceiling fan. Kodak camera. Ballpoint pen. Escalator. Zipper. Carburetor. Remote control. Who knew we had any need or use for some of these things? And once they were introduced into our lives, what more could we possibly want?

Every generation believes its visionaries and geniuses have reached the limits of innovation. And yet limits are never reached. Each new idea becomes the impetus of another idea. In fact, something new becomes the foundation for many new ideas that follow.

It appears that inventions multiply over time. Each new invention propels human thought into more than one direction and launches more and more inventions.

We tend to imagine a couple of iterations of development beyond what we have now. We can foresee new variations, improvements, or combinations of the recent inventions. The greatest visionaries imagine new concepts far beyond what already exists. However, the infinite nature of Life means that there is always even more (and more, and more, and more . . .) than what we believe is real or is possible.

Today, we can probably imagine some new ways in which laptops and smartphones will make life easier, or in which new advancements in medicine will eradicate diseases. But in the eighteenth century, no one would have imagined the existence of computers, because there was nothing in the experience of the masses (or the geniuses) from which computers would have been a natural progression. The thought of computers would have represented too much advancement beyond the eighteenth-century perspective of what was possible.

Clearly, our human brain has the capacity to imagine new ideas beyond our current experience—to a point. It seems our brain can leap only so far. But where the brain leaves off, the infinite nature of Life continues. This infinite nature of Life means that there is always more than we imagine. This "more" already exists in invisible energy. And the key to creating something new is knowing that the possibility of it already exists.

Gravity existed before Sir Isaac Newton "discovered" it in the sixteenth century. Before electricity was "discovered," the law of electricity existed. Therefore, we can assume that there are other laws that exist right now that have yet to be "discovered" and made useful to everyone. Similarly, there are other possibilities—infinite possibilities—that exist and wait to be brought from the realm of the invisible into visibility. These infinite possibilities represent ideas that are beyond our imagination at this time.

Infinite Life extends beyond our human existence and our earthly domain. It includes the visible and invisible, the actual and potential, the human construct of time and space, and the absolute in which time and space do not exist.

Infinite means that there is more to Life than we can ever imagine—no limits whatsoever. The only limits are the capacity of our human brain and of our imagination to see what is possible.

American poet and philosopher Ralph Waldo Emerson wrote that within each of us, the infinite waits "in quiet repose," and that it is *our choice* to be an inlet and an outlet to Life. It's our choice whether to make ourselves available to Life's infinite possibilities.

CONSIDER THIS

The infinite, invisible potential of Life holds every possibility to satisfy your needs and desires. Right now, the solution to your problem, the answer to your question—the way to pay your bills this week or find a new job—exists in infinite potential.

Right now the ideas, the opportunities, and everything else you require for the life you choose already exists. Your better life, your dream, lies in the invisible, waiting to be brought into visible form and experience—by you.

There is only One Life.
All of Life is where you are.
All of Life's infinite possibilities are
***your* infinite possibilities.**

Life Is Abundant

Abundance is the plentiful aspect of Life; it is more than enough of anything. Regardless of the thing being described, and regardless of the exact amount of the thing that is needed, an abundance of it is always *more than that which is needed*.

How would you like to experience abundance? If money is your desire, how much is more than what you need? Think about exactly how much money you need right now, today, and imagine having more than that. Another way to look at this is to consider whether you have plenty to share. No matter how much money you have, can you share with someone else in need? If you have plenty to share, then you have *more than that which is needed—abundance.*

> **Abun•dant, adj.**
> Possessing a more-than-adequate quantity or supply.

Are you lonely and want to experience an abundance of love? Consider what would happen if someone handed you a puppy, a kitten, or a cooing newborn baby. Would your heart open, and would you feel love? Where you previously felt devoid of love, wouldn't you suddenly feel an influx of it? Within you flows forth a wellspring of love, *more than that which is needed—abundance.*

In both examples above, the experience of abundance was generated from your own shift in awareness. Your own thought generated a shift from an experience of not enough to an experience of plenty. The experience of more love arose from your own openness to it. Abundance is the nature of Life and is plentiful at all times. Your awareness of it does not create more of it, because it already exists. Your awareness allows you to experience the abundance that is already present. Your realization of Life's bounty and your receptivity to it create the experience of it.

The ocean is abundant, yet a drop of water in the ocean does not have to find or create abundance. Within the ocean, the drop is already abundant. The drop contains all the qualities of the ocean. It does not have to try to exert itself, become exhausted, or work itself into a state of frenzy in order to experience the qualities of the ocean. Imagine this little drop thinking, *Someday, when I've worked hard enough and saved enough, I'll enjoy the abundance of the ocean. When I've raised my baby drops and they're on their own, I'll reward myself with the ocean's bounty. If all goes according to plan, I'll be floating and bobbing along effortlessly. Meanwhile, I'll satisfy myself by dreaming about the wonderful ocean as I imagine it will be . . . someday.*

The drop is immersed *in* the ocean's qualities, which include abundance. Not only is the drop not separate from the ocean, but it can never separate itself from it. Life's abundance is everywhere, and, as an inseparable part of Life, you are immersed in Life's abundance whether you have been aware of it or not.

Nowhere is Life's abundance more evident than in nature. Nature shows Life expressed in its fullness and its pure essence without any interference from humankind. The natural world is evidence that Life expresses itself in myriad and beautiful ways—abundantly. The endless fields, the majestic mountains, and the rich oceans prove Life is abundant. You needn't look far to see Life's infinite abundance. There is never a shortage of leaves on trees or blades of grass in Life's abundant nature.

The eternal cycle of Life is evidence of abundance. Consider how the death and decay of each life form represents a cycle of perpetual abundance. As the leaves of the oak tree wither and die, their debris returns to the soil to nourish it in perfect preparation for new seeds. The entire process is an endless, effortless flow toward constant, ensured production of more than enough.

As you perceive a beautiful landscape, do you realize you are part of it? You are as much a part of Life's abundance as the trees and the grass. If they are not made to struggle and strain in order to live in plenty, then neither are you. Abundance is their nature, and it is yours, too.

Life gives endlessly and abundantly. Life is always producing more than enough. This is Life's nature, and Life's nature is your nature.

CONSIDER THIS

Creating more abundance in your life doesn't have to be about working harder; rather, it is about allowing the abundance that already exists to flow through your life. Like the drop that doesn't have to try to be wet, you already live and exist in abundance.

The inherent abundance of Life is your innate inheritance. The choice of how to receive and direct your inheritance and how to participate in its activity is yours. How much abundance you experience is determined by how much you perceive, what you think you deserve, what you ask for, and what you expect.

There is no limit to how much abundance you can experience, because there is always enough—there is more than enough. There is plenty for all and plenty for you.

If you believe there is plenty, what do you desire? Can you receive it? Can you believe it?

. . . .

There is only One Life.

All of Life is where you are.

Life's infinite possibilities are your infinite possibilities.

Life's abundance means plenty for all,

plenty for you.

. . . .

Life Is Intelligent

Do you know how to grow an oak tree from an acorn? More than 73,700 websites explain how, though Life has been doing this without any instructions for centuries.

> **In•tel•li•gence, n.**
> Knowledge of information, received or imparted. The gathering or distribution of information. Evidence of order. Manifestation of a high mental capacity. The faculty of understanding.

Did you know that the earth is tilted on its axis by 23.5 degrees? This precise angle ensures the delicate and perfect balance that supports the planet. If the earth's tilt changed by even a single degree, the seasons, temperature, sunlight, and countless other variables would be altered. This seemingly small shift would throw into question how and whether life on Earth could be sustained at all. Somehow, an organizing intelligence within the whole cosmos supports our planet in the only way that makes life possible.

Even a simple paper cut is proof of universal intelligence. Without any intervention whatsoever, skin cells begin an orderly healing process. In fact, the entire human body is evidence of a naturally intelligent system that operates in every cell and organ and coordinates every function.

Life is not random and unpredictable. Despite early scientific theories, it turns out that chaos is not Life's nature—intelligent order is. Most recently, scientists who set out to confirm disorder instead found proof of order in the universe. The following simple experiment illustrates the tendency toward order.

To study order within complex systems, theoretical biologist

Stuart Kauffman created an experiment using lightbulbs. He strung two hundred lightbulbs together so that every bulb was connected to two others (randomly, not in succession). For example, lightbulb twenty-four was wired to go on if bulb fifty-eight went on, and to go off if bulb ninety-nine went on. When the entire set was turned on, various sets of bulbs went off and others went on. And so Kauffman began switching the bulbs on and off. Given that the total possible combination of on-off bulb sets was ten to the thirtieth power, he expected it to take a while for orderly sequencing to replace randomness. However, after only fourteen on-off switches, a distinct pattern emerged and repeated. Order was established and maintained.

Life's intelligence supports more Life. Intelligence is the underlying principle of wholeness and balance. It supports the natural healing process of our bodies. It constantly refreshes us with new cells every minute. It imbues the acorn with everything it needs to become an oak tree. It holds the stars in the sky and the planets in perfect orbits.

Evolution is the forward movement of Life's intelligence. The result is new paradigms, new organization, and new organisms out of that which already exists—not just new, but better. Life moves like a spiral, onward and upward, returning to its beginning. Yet it arrives not quite at the same place but at a new place—a better place.

CONSIDER THIS

You are evidence of Life's intelligence. You are not a mistake or a random occurrence. Life's intelligence within you represents infinite potential—for something new and better—from where you find yourself right now.

There is only One Life.
All of Life is where you are.
Life's infinite possibilities are
your infinite possibilities.
Life's abundance means plenty for all,
plenty for you.
Life's intelligence works *with* you and *for* you.

You are inseparable from Life. Its infinite intelligence is at your disposal. It is the source of your ideas, your inner guidance, and your intuition. Life's intelligence offers greater potential for you than you have ever known.

You are part of Life. There is more intelligence within you than you have ever experienced. If you know Life's infinite intelligence supports you, are you willing to receive more of it than you ever have before? How will you use your access to it?

Chapter 7

HOW LIFE WORKS

More Life to Experience

Before Isaac Newton discovered gravity, things that were dropped fell down and nothing that was dropped fell up. Gravity was always operative, but, once realized and understood, the principle of gravity opened vistas of possibilities to humankind.

Electricity, gravity, and other physical laws do not create *more* Life. They create more *possibilities* for Life to be expressed and experienced. There is as much Life now as before we understood electrical principles. When we understand how Life works, we can *experience more Life* than we ever have.

To a biologist, life is rich and organic. To a paleontologist, life is a progression of slow but certain change. To an ophthalmologist, life is worth seeing clearly. Ultimately, each of these scientists is looking for ways to improve, enhance, and extend life.

In the same way, each of us experiences life *according to* the perspective we look *from*. Artists see and feel beauty to be expressed.

Educators uncover knowledge to be embraced. Nurses see compassion to be shared. You can experience life from the perspective you've always had. Or you can experience life differently when you think differently about Life and about yourself.

"When you change the way you look at things, the things you look at change."

—Wayne Dwyer, author of *Wishes Fulfilled: Master the Art of Manifesting*

CONSIDER THIS

There is already all the Life there ever was and ever will be. Yet there is more for you to experience in a completely new way.

If you want to see and feel more life, you must look further and feel deeper. If you want to experience life differently, you must perceive it differently and entertain new possibilities. If you want to experience life in a different way than you ever have before, then you must think about Life in a whole new way.

Once you expand your understanding of Life, its laws, and its principles of operation, you will realize the potential of cooperating with Life to direct new possibilities to satisfy your needs and desires.

As you see that Life is with you and for you, you will appreciate the reliability and constancy of its absolute, unchanging nature. When you realize your true nature is a microcosm of Life's nature, its possibilities become your possibilities—you experience a partnership with Life. You become Life's means of new and greater expression.

Life Is Dynamic

The air around you virtually dances and sings with energy. It may not *be* form, but it is what *becomes* form. It is from this rich energy that your better life will take form.

Energy is the building block, the substance, and the power of the universe. Everything is composed of energy; energy is omnipresent.

> **Dy•nam•ic, adj.**
> Pertaining to energy, activity, action. Force that produces motion.

Matter and all form is energy that is in constant motion, or vibration. Particular forms of matter are the result of specific combinations of molecules and a specific rate of vibration of energy.

Even forms that appear to be completely lifeless, such as rocks and minerals, contain energy. In unscientific terms, rocks are vibrating at such a low frequency that they appear solid and unmoving. The pattern of vibration is what determines the form energy takes.

ENERGY FACTS

Einstein discovered that energy and matter are forms of the same thing. Matter can be turned into energy; energy can become matter.

In physics, the law of conservation states that energy is never lost, only transformed into new forms.

But where does all form come from? Since all of Life already exists, then everything is either form or formless, visible or invisible, actual or potential. Therefore, all visible material form was once invisible potential energy.

Let's use a coffee mug as a simple example. Your coffee mug is vibrating energy, but it originated as potential energy. Once upon a time, it was only a thought in the mind of a product designer who was receptive to a new product-design idea. This idea set in motion new possibilities (in manufacturing and distribution, for instance) that eventually resulted in the mug that's sitting on your desk. However you look at it—potential energy became a mug, or the mug began as potential energy—energy is the building block of all form. An oak tree began as potential energy within the acorn that produced it; conversely, the acorn began as potential energy within the oak tree that produced it.

Did you know that any particle of matter contains more space than matter itself? In other words, all solid form is mostly empty space. So it's easy to understand that there is more invisible energy than visible energy that has already taken form in our world. For the purposes of creativity, let's call all invisible energy either potential form or possibility of form. Therefore, there is more potential or possibility than what we perceive as solid matter or real experience.

There is more Life than you know and more than you can imagine.

This is not an essay on science. It is an explanation of a basic concept with profound implications for you—that all form is energy being expressed. The infinite wellspring of unformed energy contains every possibility. And you play a significant role in directing the form Life's dynamic energy takes in your life.

CONSIDER THIS

The question isn't whether you use Life's energy, because it is impossible to separate yourself from it. You direct energy when you put your attention into a new project, use your imagination, and say yes to anything.

You can make use of the energy that powers your own body and everything else. You can take advantage of Life's dynamic nature, because it is *your* nature. You can harness this power to change your experience of life, to fuel your greatest dreams, and to participate in a world that longs for your dreams.

Energy molds to the pattern and direction you give it. The question is, how will you use it?

Life's dynamic energy vibrates *through* you.

Life Is Expressive

All invisible energy is form that has yet to be expressed or form that is in the process of finding expression. Life's expressive nature turns possibilities into form. Seeds sprout. Sunrises emerge. Rivers change course. A new job opens up. A friend introduces you to someone new. An unexpected gift arrives.

In fact, Life is unstoppable in bringing more and more potential into actuality. No two snowflakes are alike. The sunset paints the sky brilliantly and completely differently each evening. There are 23,600 species in the daisy flowering-plant family alone!

Life's expressive nature also includes new possibilities that require you and me. Life truly needs us to express into form new possibilities that are conceivable only because of us. Ideas, inventions, discoveries, technology, and all artistic forms couldn't happen without our ability to think and to choose. Our thoughts become the mold for Life to fill for the expression of something new.

We're not a by-product. We're a vital part of Life's abundance, intelligence, expression, creativity, and flow. We are an essential component of Life's dynamic, expressive, and creative operation.

CONSIDER THIS

Are you willing to participate with Life and become receptive to its infinite potential? There are possibilities with your name on them, waiting for you to invite them into creation.

When you understand your vital and inseparable relationship with Life—that you are Life being expressed—you realize that it is you who opens the doors to your dreams. You are the way potential becomes real and possibilities become actualities.

The solution to your current challenge already exists. The right words you need to express the thought you want to communicate roll off your tongue. The perfect ending to your novel is available to you. The opportunity that brings everything together for you is yours. The right person who can help you achieve your goal awaits you. The next step toward manifesting your new idea already exists.

When you understand the creative process of Life, you will be able to bring into form new ideas that would not be possible without you. You will finally understand and experience how much you matter to Life.

Life's dynamic energy vibrates through you.
Life's expressive nature *requires* you.

Life Is Responsive

Life is not one-directional. There is a back-and-forth, a give-and-take, a dance between Life and everything it creates. Life's abundance ensures there is always plenty of everything to support every need, answer every problem, and manifest every dream. Life's responsiveness is what fills the need, answers the problems, and actualizes the dream.

The seasons are Life's response to the needs of plant and animal life. Rain is Life's gift to parched land. The interconnectedness of all life forms shows how Life provides for the needs of all that it creates.

Let's look at an example. A seed planted in soil receives all that it needs to grow and sprout, to thrive, and to mature into a fully developed plant. Life provides the sun, the rain, the nutrients, and everything the seed needs to become the expression of a tree, shrub, or flowering plant, etc.

Likewise, Life provides everything our human bodies require to thrive. Life provides air, water, and nutrition to sustain our bodies. The capability to reproduce, incubate our seedlings, and bring forth new expressions of Life is built in.

Life creates and responds—to what is created—in order to express more and more of itself. Remember, there is always all of Life already. However, *more life* refers to new expression and new experience of Life from invisible potential.

Our thoughts bring Life's possibilities into form. Thoughts

are seeds. Like the soil, Life's invisible creative medium nurtures, feeds, and matures our thoughts into things and our possibilities into realities. From the seed of our thoughts, form and experience sprout forth and blossom. The responsive nature of Life makes it possible.

CONSIDER THIS

Life responds to you because it is part of you. It responds to your thoughts, words, and deeds. It responds in a perfect, reliable, and consistent way. Life does not play favorites or play games by being erratic or unreliable.

When another heart touches our own, the compassion we feel is Life responding to Life. When the needs of another pull us irresistibly to share what we have with them and help them, Life is responding to Life. When our intuition guides us to be in a certain place or do a certain thing without realizing the perfect synchronicity, Life is responding to Life (i.e., itself in you).

Life's responsiveness makes it your dependable partner for co-creation. You can plant the seeds of your desire and cultivate them into something new.

Life's dynamic energy vibrates through you.
Life's expressive nature requires you.
Life's responsiveness works *with* you.

Life Is Giving, Flowing, Circulating. Life Is Good.

Life moves in the direction of creating and supporting more. As it creates more, it doesn't repeat itself but builds upon itself and uses what it creates to express more. Like a spiral that returns never to the same place but to a fresh beginning, Life perpetually supports more and more. Life's inherent tendency is toward new, higher, and better—Life is good.

The cycle of Life in all forms expresses its nature toward more Life—Life is good. Life's nature is to create in ways that are Life-affirming, rather than Life-depleting—Life is good. Life expresses in a perfect and balanced way—Life is good.

This constant creative nature is giving because Life gives from its infinite, bottomless potential into new form and new experience. It is flowing because its constant creativity is unimpeded, with no resistance, no beginning, and no ending. It is circulating because Life's energy connects and moves through everything.

Life's qualities—beauty, harmony, abundance, and so forth—are always and immeasurably available. Our awareness of them ensures their circulation, flow, and expansion. As we give our attention to anything, our energy vibration begins to resonate with it and add to it. All of this combined energy becomes like a vortex, which emanates and attracts forms and experiences of like energy. Therefore, we become part of Life's flowing circulation of good.

Circulation is important because it ensures the expression of more Life. Without circulation, living forms stagnate. To illustrate this concept, try holding your breath as you read this. Keep holding. Holding. Okay, please breathe now! Can you see that as you prevented the natural circulation of air in your lungs, your body was no longer able to receive the vital life energy it needed to survive and thrive? Circulation of air is your main life support. Consider how many other functions within your body require circulation: blood flow, glandular secretions, etc.

In the same way, a pond needs circulation in order for every living thing in it and around it to thrive. Without sufficient flow of oxygen and nutrients, the pond would stagnate and its inhabitants would suffer as the balance of life within it was disrupted.

All of Life's nature is good, and the cycle of Life is good. Life does not express depletion, death, and deterioration. (It may seem so, but in the big picture, death and destruction appear as part of a cycle that ultimately affirms more Life, not less.) There is no death but simply a change of form, since nothing ever leaves the omnipresence of Life. (Science tells us that energy is never lost in the universe but merely changes form.)

Even as flowers "die," they are forever part of a vast, complex, and interconnected system. Life continues as the seed of a flower becomes not just one new flower, but the seeds of many flowers. Most animals produce more than one offspring per animal, thus demonstrating the nature of Life to expand and to express more life.

Recall the earlier example of how new inventions led to the exponential growth of more inventions; history shows that there is more Life than we can ever conceive, and its nature is expansive. The tendency of Life to dynamically respond to its own expressions in ways that are expansive and abundant, thereby multiplying the expression of Life in form, is what we call giving. After all, a giving nature (whether it is our own or the nature of Life) is evidence of plenty.

Where do catastrophes, loss, and disasters fit into this "good" and "giving" system of Life? In the grand scheme, there is more good than bad. It is easier to understand why this is so if we momentarily magnify this statement: there are more amazingly great things happening than unthinkable catastrophes. If there were not, this universe would not exist. The catastrophic would eventually obliterate the amazingly good.

Life's infinite abundance guarantees that there is no end to its gifts, no limit to the good available to you.

CONSIDER THIS

The nature of Life is giving and good, and it is your nature, too. Life is your partner, and when you partner with Life, it gives infinite good to you. Every good you desire is available to you.

No matter how anything appears, it is never devoid of Life's good. Good is always present. It's as sure as the sun on an overcast day. Even when you cannot see good, rest assured it is there, even if only as potential—for good that is becoming.

When you start looking for the good, the potential, the possibilities, you will realize that what you are seeking is also seeking you.

Life's dynamic energy vibrates through you.
Life's expressive nature requires you.
Life's responsiveness works with you.
Life's flow offers more good *to you* and
through you.

Principles and Laws

Principles and laws describe what Life is and how Life works.

A principle is a fundamental truth about Life. It is absolute and universal because it applies to every condition and situation. A principle is nothing more than a statement of what is, indisputably. Life is omnipresent. Life is infinite. Life is abundant. Life is intelligent.

A law describes an action or how things work. Laws are as precise as mathematical equations like $2 + 2 = 4$. They are infallible, universal, constant, and impersonal. To use the laws that govern your life to enhance your life, you must understand why the properties of laws are important. Let's use the example of electricity to illustrate the properties of laws.

Law property #1: Laws are definite. Laws are a formula, a key to how things work. If they were not, how could anyone use them? Laws provide equations that can be applied to many things. If not for the definite, formulaic nature of physical laws, Thomas Edison and every other inventor wouldn't have gotten anywhere.

Law property #2: Laws are infallible. They work all the time. They never slack off or take a day off. The invisible laws that make electricity possible are always in effect. Nothing needs to be done in order to activate the orbit of electrons around the nuclei of atoms. Electrons never rest.

Law property #3: Laws are universal. They operate under every condition and apply to every part of Life. The universal law of electricity works exactly the same way in the field of computer technology as it does in the field of medicine. The same principles that make a light-bulb shine also make it possible to cauterize a blood vessel.

Law property #4: Laws are constant. They are always in operation and never change. Never. Using the laws of electricity, we can create artificial light, power inanimate objects, provide our homes with heat or air-conditioning, or power televisions.

Law property #5: Laws are impersonal. They favor no one. No matter who uses it, how they use it, or even if they are aware or ignorant of it, the law does what it does. Laws don't even care if love or hate motivates our use of them. Our use of laws may create or destroy, but the law itself does not.

> "There is no limit to the Law, but there appears to be a limit to man's understanding of it. The thing that makes us sick is the thing that heals us."
> —Ernest Holmes, *The Science of Mind*

We can use electricity for positive or destructive purposes. Misuse or complete ignorance of electricity can electrocute, incinerate, and cause great harm and destruction. The law of electricity does not guarantee benefits or prevent catastrophe—knowledge and intention do.

Being ignorant of laws does not stop its action or its effect on us. However, understanding laws enables us to use them for a specific purpose and personal benefit. Realizing that Life works in certain ways that support you will help you change, re-create, redesign, or reinvent your life, from what you do not want to what you really want.

Everything According to Law

Physical laws describe the activity of visible energy: the law of thermo-dynamics, the law of gravity. Universal laws govern and operate how Life works all the time and includes both the visible *and* the invisible.

As scientists discover more laws of physics, chemistry, and the physical world, more laws are named. Similarly, as we understand how the invisible world of potential operates, we formulate laws to describe them. Here are a few of them. Each one follows the five properties of law.

> **Law.**
> Generic use of the word "law" refers to the auto-matic operation of cause and effect—an impetus produces a corresponding effect.

Law of creation: Everything is created through a process that manifests visible matter and experience from an infinite field of in-visible energy.

Law of cause and effect: Everything in form and experience (effect) originates from consciousness intelligence (cause).

Law of circulation: Life operates by dynamic, perpetual activity in which energy (or the "effect" of energy) is always in motion, never lost but rather transformed.

Law of increase: Life creates new forms and experiences in a pat-tern of advancement and growth, always to express more of itself.

Law of attraction: Like attracts like. Positive energy attracts more positive energy. Negative energy attracts more negative energy. No matter how any form of energy vibrates, it tends to match similar vibration levels.

The laws named here are some important ones that reveal the process by which the invisible becomes visible: the law of cause and effect, the law of circulation, the law of growth. Even a cursory understanding of these laws will allow you to manage your life better.

No matter how many laws have been named or are yet to be, the common denominator of all laws is the irrefutable truth that Life works according to law. There is an orderly pattern of intelligence that governs the creation, maintenance, and growth of all forms of Life. We may continue to define its countless nuances of operation, but we must recognize, respect, and understand that Life works according to law.

For our purposes here, know that anything that becomes form from the invisible does so through the activity of creative law. Throughout this book, the word "law" is used to denote Life's automatic production of effect according to cause.

Personal Law

You can't stop a river from flowing, but you can change your own place in the river so you'll be carried *with* it. You cannot change the nature of the sun to radiate, but you can stay out of the sun to preserve your skin, or you can harness its energy to warm your home.

A personal law is simply your individual use of the universal law that governs the transformation of invisible energy into visible form and experience. As everything that is visible comes from invisible energy, everything in your life is created by thought.

As it is easier to observe this activity in the lives of others than in our own, try this exercise: Become a neutral observer of how laws operate for other people. Do you know people who seem to have bad luck and whom a dark cloud seems to follow wherever they go? Mishaps, problems, accidents, and hardships are their way of life. Can you identify their thoughts and beliefs by how they speak about Life? Can you see the personal effects they have created?

Do you know people who glide through life as though they are charmed and lucky? Everything goes their way. Everyone cooperates with them, and everything works smoothly for them. Do you think they believe in a friendly or unfriendly universe? What do you observe about their way of thinking relative to mass media and the collective opinion of others?

The laws that govern your life have no agenda for you. They either help or hinder your life according to your use (or unknowing misuse) of them. Without knowing it, you may be using Life's universal laws in ways that are producing the exact experience you don't want. In other words, you may be working against Life's laws instead of with them. Laws do not limit you; your use of them does.

Used rightly, laws will help you make your life work better. Laws support expansion, abundance, order, harmony, and every other quality of Life you choose to experience. It is up to you to use them to your greatest benefit. Laws provide limitless opportunities for you.

Your personal use of universal laws dictates how Life operates *specifically for you* based on your specific beliefs about Life. Your thoughts, beliefs, attitudes, and general mental atmosphere lay the groundwork for the immutable action of Life's law(s). Your thoughts supply the "cause" from which an "effect" is produced.

In fact, it is your use of universal laws that creates your experience, whether you experience wealth or poverty, love or loneliness. If you constantly think of lack, limitation, and insufficiency of money to meet your obligations, in essence you operate under a "law of poverty" that you created. If you worry and fear you will never find your soul mate, you are creating a "law of loneliness." If you accept the consensus of disaster, drama, and doom, it may seem like the "law of waiting-for-the-other-shoe-to-drop." These three examples aren't actual laws; they're laws you create with your own way of thinking. Most important, they create your experience, which *is* real.

"There is no such thing as a lack of faith. We all have plenty of faith; it's just that we have faith in the wrong things. We have faith in what can't be done rather than what can be done. We have faith in lack rather than abundance, but there is no lack of faith. Faith is a law."
—Eric Butterworth, author of thirteen-plus books on positive and prosperous living

Universal law does not produce good or bad conditions. It produces according to the thoughts and beliefs in your consciousness. Your consciousness contains what you've accepted as well as what you've allowed by default (sometimes the beliefs of others). The nature of Life (to produce according to your thought) does not change. But *you* can.

CONSIDER THIS

You create your own laws by what you choose to think and believe. Choose a law of prosperity instead of a law of poverty, a law of lovableness instead of a law of loneliness. Opt out of the consensus of expecting life to be hard and create your own law of ease and grace. Stop accepting Murphy's Law that if something bad can happen, it will happen, and replace it with a possibility law that if something better can happen, it will.

You can choose whether to experience Life as friendly or unfriendly, Life as a series of miracles or setbacks, or Life worth living or leaving.

Chapter 8

LIFE IS FOR YOU (BECAUSE IT NEEDS YOU)

HUMANS PLAY AN IMPORTANT ROLE in the spiral of Life's nature to express more and more Life. We are the apex of Life's expression and unbounded potential. Why? Because we have the capacity for conscious thought and free will. This unique capacity sets us apart from any other form of life. While animals act instinctively in order to survive, free will allows us to act from volition that is not dependent solely on survival.

If our unique capacity of thinking empowers unique possibilities, then *we* must serve a unique purpose. If thought and volition are necessary for new possibilities of Life's expression, then *we* must play an important role in the creative process that brings new things into form.

Clearly, some ideas would remain in the field of potential energy if they did not have an outlet for expression. The ceiling of the Sistine Chapel would be ordinary plaster if not for Michelangelo. "Happy Birthday" would be only a statement and not a song. Our capacity for thought makes us perfectly suited to bring invisible possibilities into form. It is as though we are the mold maker, because through our thoughts and beliefs, new possibilities become actualities.

Of course, in order to manifest new possibilities, we must understand our role in the creative process and choose to participate with Life in it. Once we recognize the limitless potential in this partnership, we can begin to solve our problems and realize our greatest desires.

CONSIDER THIS

You make new expressions of Life possible. You play an important role in Life's creative process. Ideas, possibilities, and opportunities remain in the field of potential energy if they do not have a means to manifest them—you.

The possibility for your answers, your solutions, and something new and better exists and awaits your invitation into actuality. What else would you choose to welcome into the world? Infinite possibilities are ready. The next great novel—why not you? The way to peace—why not you?

The Creative Process

When Life's dynamic, expressive energy is directed with purpose, something creative happens. A creative process produces all things and experience. Without this process, virtually everything would remain in the field of infinite possibilities.

All forms of life—trees, rivers, oceans, flowers—are evidence of the creative process in the natural physical world. This same process also results in everything else in the world, from coffee mugs to rocket ships, from first dates to career achievements.

Everything that becomes form and experience does so through the creative process. Everything that is already in your life, as well as everything that is being created right now in your life, happens through this process.

The building blocks of creativity include thought, belief, ideas, imagination, and intuition. Each of these will be explained and put in the context of the creative process soon. For now, it is important to understand what the process is and how it fits into Life's nature (what Life is and how Life works).

Realize that the process that creates the stars and the planets and holds them in perfect orbit is the same process that produces absolutely everything. Can you begin to imagine how you can use it to create what you desire?

The creative process has three basic components: What Life is, how Life works, and what Life becomes. Everything that is made or experienced includes these components. It doesn't matter if something exists by nature or by way of conscious thought and human hands—this creative process is the means by which it came to be.

Remember the qualities of what Life is?

Life is everywhere.

Life is infinite.

Life is abundant.

Life is intelligent.

These qualities describe the source of everything, the repository of infinite potential that becomes real. This is the first part of creativity: the infinite source of possibilities.

Remember the qualities of how Life works?

Life is dynamic.

Life is expressive.

Life is responsive.

Life is giving, flowing, circulating—good.

Life is in constant operation that yields new creative forms and experience. These properties of Life's activity comprise the second component of creativity: the properties of Life's creativity.

The third part of the creative process is the actual form or experience. It is the visible that bursts from the invisible. It is a thing that originally was not a thing but the potential of the thing. It is everything around you—the computer on your desk, your kid's backpack, the painting on your wall.

The creative process can be summarized like this:

WHAT LIFE IS	Everywhere. Infinite. Abundant. Intelligent.
HOW LIFE WORKS	Dynamic. Expressive. Responsive. Good.
WHAT LIFE BECOMES	Form. Experience

The seed, soil, and plant provide a simple illustration of Life's creative process and the operation of its powerful laws. The seed represents the impetus of new life, and within the seed is everything necessary to produce the exact form of life it represents. The acorn contains the blueprint for its complete success as a mighty oak. The soil transforms the seed, providing the perfect incubation and nourishment to bring forth the plant.

The seed represents the spark of possibility. The soil demonstrates Life's responsive nature to act upon the seed and provide everything for its growth. The plant is the full expression of the seed, corresponding exactly to the original blueprint of possibility within it.

WHAT LIFE IS	SEED
Everywhere. Infinite. Abundant. Intelligent.	Life's nature
HOW LIFE WORKS	**SOIL**
Dynamic. Expressive. Responsive. Good.	Life's creative operation
WHAT LIFE BECOMES	**PLANT**
Form. Experience.	Life's expression

This process creates everything, from possibility through creativity into form. All form and experience originates with a seed that contains its blueprint or pattern of growth. The computer on your desk began as an idea. The rocket ship also originated as a thought, an idea, and an inspiration.

Creativity Is Now

The dynamic nature of Life means creativity is always happening, something new is always coming into form. Yet, it's important to realize that creativity happens only in the present and never in the past or in the future.

> "What lies behind us and what lies before us are tiny matters compared to what lies within us."
>
> —Ralph Waldo Emerson, poet, essayist, philosopher

It is obvious that you cannot change any facts of the past, and it is obvious that you cannot create anything in the future. However, the obvious is worth stating because it is so easy to replay the past and consider all the different ways it could have played out. It is just as easy to dream about all the infinite futures you can experience.

How often do your waking thoughts include thoughts about your past or your future? Thinking about the past is important only as far as it informs, motivates, and directs your thoughts right now as part of the process of creating a new experience. Thoughts about the past can be comforting when they are Life-affirming and useful to your creativity right now.

When Life-draining thoughts of the past stir up regret, blame, shame, and guilt, you must realize that those thoughts are creative, too. The creative process is always at work, but not always in the direction of what you want. It is invaluable to rid yourself of shame, blame, regret, and guilt.

It can be valuable to understand the choices you've made and their consequences, in order to see the path that brought you to where you are today. Revisiting past experiences with new wisdom can help change your perspective on them. For example, if you have a pattern of picking unsuitable romantic partners, analyzing what works and what doesn't is time well spent in creating a new intention for finding and attracting your perfect mate.

A healthy inquiry into the past can empower better choices. No one has ever changed the past. But you can change your perception of it, the meaning you have assigned to it, and its impact on your current state of mind and emotions.

Similarly, you cannot create in the future. You might worry about how things will turn out, but worry indicates fear and doubt. These kinds of thoughts reveal lack of understanding or faith that you are creating your new future right now. They mislead you to think you have no control, your choices don't matter, and even *you* don't matter in how your life is going to unfold. Worry, fear, and doubt are all counterproductive to what you want to create now.

You can have positive thoughts of the future, visualize what you want, and entertain your greatest dreams. Positive energy is conducive to setting goals and intentions that get you excited about your better future. Still, the *now* moment holds the key to creating it.

Creativity happens only in the present, and the present is rich with creativity. So anytime your attention is not in the present moment, you are neglecting (whether consciously or unconsciously) the amazing potential that is with you *right now*.

In the present moment, you can change your path *from the past* or establish a new course *toward the future* you desire. This is the way the next (potential) moment becomes the now reality. What truly matters is creating something new, now.

> "Within you is a limitless, unborn potential of creativity and substance, and the present experience can be your great opportunity to give birth to it."
> —Eric Butterworth, author of *Discover the Power Within You*

Creativity Is Your Ally

If you can think of it, you can plant the seed of it.

In order to release the talents and potential for fulfillment that Life implanted within you, you must participate with Life. It doesn't matter whether you want to alleviate the experience of suffering right now or to achieve your highest goals. You will experience something better as you become the willing, cooperative, and active seed of something better.

Partnership with Life depends on you. Thought takes you over the threshold into Life's infinite possibilities.

Thought is the energy of human consciousness. It is the mental activity and movement of Life energy within us. Thought energy (i.e., the specific pattern or vibration of your thoughts) attracts other like energy. In other words, a vibration of positive thought attracts things and experiences that are perceived as positive. Likewise, negative thought attracts negative forms and experience.

Life responds and acts upon your thoughts as the soil acts upon the seed, gathering and attracting to it everything it requires for nourishment and growth. Life responds *to you* as you think, according to the pattern of your thought. Life also provides *for you* according to your thought energy. If you are open to new ideas, new ideas become available to you. If you make yourself available to new possibilities, your imagination will become alive with possibility. If you become aware of your unity with infinite intelligence, your intuition can become a perfect guidance system.

That each person is a completely unique and unrepeatable expression of Life is evidence that we are Life's insurance against reaching a dead end. As long as there are unique people, there will be an exponentially greater variety in the way Life is expressed.

You are the universe, expressing itself as a human for a little while."

—Eckhart Tolle, author of *The Power of Now*

Life is for you because you are a necessary part of its expressive nature. Life will respond to you *as you choose*. You determine how Life will be expressed *through you*, and Life will respond with corresponding form and experience *for you*.

Life desires for you whatever you desire for yourself.

The creative process is in constant operation, with no beginning and no end. Whatever becomes form and experience is simply a new impetus for more new form and experience. For example, once the computer was invented, it served as a launching point for endless technology and products. Similarly, your experience of something new will lead you to new goals and dreams. In this way, Life's dynamic nature is reflected in the creative process. It is the law of circulation illustrated: endless creation, with no beginning and no end, like Life itself.

The creative process ensures continuous, uninterrupted expression of more Life. Unique form and experience are produced because of our own unique energy, thoughts, and beliefs. The same thought that occurs to you will have entirely different consequences if thought by someone else.

What you think about, you create.
What you put your attention on expands.
What you resist persists.

Whether you are aware of it or not, you are co-creating (because it's a partnership) your life right now. You can see everything in your life as the effect of creativity that gets its impetus from you. Your attention sets the direction of creativity. Therefore, if you put your attention on what you don't want, you vibrate at the frequency of it, you emanate it—and you attract more of it.

When your energy is vibrating in a pattern that matches what you *do* want, what you want will become attracted to you. The way to do this is to change your thoughts and beliefs so their energy patterns are conducive to the new form and experience you want.

If you want to attract love in your life, you must already *have the energy of love*. Do this by believing in the possibility of love, showing what a loving person you are, celebrating love wherever you notice it (and noticing it more). If you want a more fulfilling career, you must create *the energy that matches it*. Start by believing it is possible, visualizing your perfect career, anticipating various ways it will enhance your life, and talk to others who are fulfilled by their work.

See how both of these examples change the pattern of your energy because you are aligning your attention, your thoughts, and your beliefs *with* what you want? The point is to create a shift in you that will activate something new.

Let's look at these examples in the creative process:

SEED	Plant the seeds of desire and intention. A new love. A better job.
SOIL	Match thoughts, beliefs, energy and expections to what you want. Life's creativity responds to you.
PLANT	Life produces new form and experience. Introductions. Opportunities. New ideas. Maybe something better…

If you want something better than what is, you must cultivate what you want. Creative geniuses make themselves receptive to new ideas, not existing ones. Inventors focus on what's possible, not on what already is.

Ideas, Imagination, and Intuition

Ideas, imagination, and intuition represent the workshop, the playground, and the library of Life's seeds of infinite possibility. Every product, invention, and advancement in technology begins as an idea, a seed of manifestation. And what you desire is the seed of a new experience.

"All achievements, all earned riches, have their beginning in an idea."
—Napoleon Hill, *Think and Grow Rich*

As plants produce seeds that are dispersed into the world to further secure their continued existence, Life furthers its expression via the seeds of thought. Imagination is how Life disperses the seeds of new ideas. Imagination is how you cultivate ideas.

Idea: a concept. Ideas can be general (I'm going to take up art) or specific (I have the engineering solution for this problem).

Imagination: our link to Life's infinite potential. Thought and ideas that stimulate awareness of possibilities.

Intuition: direct contact with Life's intelligence. Heightened awareness of knowing without reason or explanation. Sensed as inner guidance toward what is Life-affirming (e.g. the right choice, decision, or path in a situation) or Life-depleting (e.g. intuiting impending danger in a stranger or situation).

Intuition is an inner sense of direct contact with something greater than you—Life. Intuition is like having access to a library of everything known and unknown. It can be experienced as a sort of coaching system: go here, or do not go there, or here's what you need to know now. Intuition is a felt sense of guidance and support. Often called "the still, small voice within," intuition is a result of your own receptivity to Life's wisdom and intelligence. If you keep your attention on it, Life will respond to you because its nature is to respond.

For our purposes, it's not important to make fine distinctions between ideas, imagination, and intuition, because they come from the same source. What's important is to recognize their great significance in the process of creativity.

Imagination has often been treated as a frivolous luxury of children and artists. It is both of these things and yet indescribably more. If frivolity suggests playfulness, imagination does require lightness of being for its playground. A playful imagination taps into the source of infinite possibilities. Imagining possibilities is playing with Life and letting Life play with you. Instead of being a luxury, imagination is truly a rich and exciting expression of Life's infinite abundance. The world's greatest thinkers recognize that imagination leads to ideas, and ideas can lead you along an amazing new path.

"Imagination is more important than knowledge."
—Albert Einstein

Our minds are inseparably connected to the infinite field of Life—its giving, responsive, and dynamic nature. It *gives us* new inspiration. It *responds* to our desire with imagined possibilities. It *constantly* creates the world around us according to the thoughts we entertain. Our life becomes what we believe. Every possibility that becomes our reality must be planted as a seed (of thought), and thoughts are stimulated by ideas, imagination, and intuition. As you cultivate ideas, Life's creativity does its part to provide for their manifestation.

> **Life gives you ideas seeking expression. This is more valuable than any single thing you can imagine.**

Thoughts and Beliefs Are Creative

Scientists have shown that everything, including our thoughts, vibrates at certain frequency levels. Negative thoughts vibrate at specific frequency levels, and positive thoughts vibrate at specific frequency levels, and these levels are very different from each other.

The law of attraction states that things of a certain energy vibration attract other things with a similar, matching vibration—like attracts like. This is also called resonance, when the vibration of one thing activates the vibration of another thing because the specific pattern of their vibration matches.

Here is an illustration of resonance as an attracting energy. If two guitars are tuned precisely the same, and one string on the first guitar is plucked in close proximity to the same string on the second guitar, the second string will begin vibrating of its own accord. This is because each string has a tendency (because of its particular

Thought: mental activity. Conscious thought is movement of energy that the thinker senses as distinct ideas or a stream of concepts. Subconscious thought is mental activity without awareness by the thinker.

Belief: a pattern of thought. What you have conviction about; what you think is true. Beliefs can be negative or positive, or degrees in between. Not to be confused with faith or certainty. Faith is a belief in something (and not the lack of it), without needing evidence for it. Certainty is confidence born from evidence or logical deduction.

Resonance: the activation of vibration of an object or system when exposed to a force whose frequency is equal or close to the frequency of the object or system.

tuning) to vibrate at a certain level. The playing of one activates the tendency in the other.

We experience this same property of resonance when we are in close proximity to another person whose energy affects ours. Have you ever noticed when someone's positive energy lifts your inner vibration or when someone's dark cloud of despair seems to become your dark cloud of despair? Resonance requires the affected object, or person, to exist in a vibration close to the first one's. So it stands to reason that we either pick up the vibration of another or resonate with people who share our own vibration.

Thought is energy that also has a specific vibrational frequency, and this energy is a powerful creator of our life experience. Scientists tell us we have more than sixty thousand thoughts a day. Sixty thousand! While you may not be fully aware of all of them, you are likely aware that some are empowering thoughts and others are not. The creative process governs all of your thoughts. Fortunately, your experience is the result of the *majority* of your thoughts, the vibration established by the *predominance* of your thoughts.

It is a gross generalization that positive, empowering, Life-affirming beliefs yield only positive, happy, and creative experiences, while negative, limited, invalidating, and Life-draining beliefs cause only unhappy, meager experiences. You have a lot of positive and negative thoughts; you are confident about some parts of your life and fearful about others. Your mindset (or consciousness) is the sum of all of these, and it is a powerful causative factor in how you experience your life.

Think about whether you have been operating under the assumption that your life today is the result of circumstances, influences, the decisions of others, or anything outside you and your own thoughts. To some, the realization that your thoughts are creating your life might be a shocking revelation. Your response may be, "You mean I *created* my terrible circumstances, my disease, the fact that I have no partner, that I can't afford to pay my bills . . . ?" Since the purpose of this book is to simplify complex concepts, the simple answer is yes—your thoughts have helped create your current experience. Nevertheless, the *more important* thing to remember is that *anything can be changed to something better.*

Regardless of your circumstance, thought played a part in creating it, and thought can change it. It doesn't matter whether you constantly thought of the negative things that came to be or whether these thoughts (maybe from others, maybe from accepted public opinion) slipped by you unnoticed and became your thoughts—and your experience—because the more important, and more promising, idea is that *something better is possible.*

Since this is a challenging topic for many, let's illustrate how it *might* work in a way that we can understand without being thrown into a tailspin of blame and guilt. Because people are living longer in our current society, certain "conditions" of aging have become the norm. It's common to fear and also to expect many people to be diagnosed with dementia or Alzheimer's disease. In my own experience with my mother's Alzheimer's, I noticed a level of fear in everyone involved, including me. My awareness allowed me to make a powerful choice in shifting my thoughts to create new possibilities.

Using the example of Alzheimer's, think of how much attention and thought are given to these conditions. Think of how these conditions are becoming more prevalent. Can you consider the possibility that the increased thoughts about these conditions might be helping to create them? Now, in your own life, can you think of something you dreaded and feared that eventually became real?

Again, not every thought manifests itself. *That person doesn't like me* is a single thought that may have little impact on your life. However, *I'm not lovable* is a belief, a pattern of thoughts that is born out of real or perceived experiences. This mindset of "unlovable" will create experiences of being unlovable, some of which might be real and some of which you might simply perceive this way. The point is, the experience will continue until the belief that is creating it is changed.

Understanding that your thoughts are creative lets you take responsibility for what is being created and empowers you to create something else. Your thoughts have power; align them with what you want, not with what you don't want.

"You are responsible for the energy that you create for yourself, and you're responsible for the energy that you bring to others."
—Oprah Winfrey

Realizing that your thought is powerful is realizing that *you* are powerful. This can relieve you from feeling victimized by circumstances and other people. If you can direct the course of your life, you can realize the potential for change. You can become hopeful that you can end your suffering, scarcity of good, and the feeling of being powerless. In fact, you can eliminate the thought that you are a victim of anything or anyone.

What about situations in which another person really is in control? What can thinking differently accomplish? There are countless war stories in which prisoners make a conscious decision not to accept the thought of being a victim and thereby reclaim a state of mental freedom that change their experience of imprisonment or lead to their release. One news story featured a woman threatened at gunpoint who decided to show compassion to her aggressor. She believed it ultimately influenced his intention and saved her life. These examples illustrate that thought is not only the first step but also sometimes the only way out of victimhood.

"So I tried not to spend my time asking, 'Why did this happen to me?' but trying to figure out why I had chosen this."
—Oprah Winfrey

A word of caution is in order here. Don't go overboard and heap inordinate blame on yourself for everything in your life. Accepting responsibility can be a powerful motivator to change. Accepting blame (or shame or regret) can be counterproductive if it immobilizes you to change. Furthermore, blame, shame, and regret cultivate negative energy and Life-draining thoughts that will contribute to creating more of the same. Realize, however, that blame, shame, and regret are thoughts and beliefs, which can be changed, released, and transformed.

Create a New Mold

Imagine a liquid substance being poured into a mold. The mold determines the final form of the substance. Thoughts provide the mold for new forms.

Seed ideas and inspiration activate the energy of possibilities. Your thoughts, beliefs, attitudes, and feelings create a mold that specializes this energy for you. The resulting unique form or experience corresponds to your unique thoughts and beliefs. Therefore, several people may have the same original idea, but by the time the idea is created into something, it has the distinctive stamp of the person who ushered it into something fresh and new.

You may recall the movie *Big*, in which Tom Hanks's character trades bodies with a child. But did you also know that four other movies with the same concept were released close to the same time? This shows how an idea, available to anyone receptive to it, finds a suitable receptive mind for it. Each person's particular mold of thinking specialized the idea into a unique and distinct execution. Have you ever seen one of your ideas eventually produced by someone else and said, "Hey, I thought of that!"? Infinite ideas are available to everyone, yet each person's unique thoughts determine what ideas they receive and how they express them.

You, your thoughts, and what they create are one of a kind. Are you beginning to appreciate that what makes you special is what makes you matter? Your uniqueness fulfills Life's nature to express something new, which is possible only because of you.

> "I paint objects as I think them, not as I see them."
> —Pablo Picasso

Belief Determines Experience

Patterns of thought become beliefs, some of which you are aware of and some of which you are not. Beliefs work for you when they create things and experiences that are agreeable to you, and they work against you when the result is what you don't want.

What do you believe about the world, about Life, and about yourself? Once again, do you believe you live in a friendly universe or an unfriendly one? How full is your glass? Everything you think, say, or do reflects your belief system. If it's difficult to see your own beliefs in action, it might be easier to observe how beliefs work for someone else.

YOUR BELIEFS
Continue to journal about your beliefs.

NEW CHOICES
Continue to reexamine what you have believed up until now, as well as what you choose to believe from this point on.

You probably know someone who always wants to tell you about the worst thing they read in yesterday's news. Their commentary often begins with, "Did you hear what happened?" and ends with, "Can you believe what they did?" There might be many good things in their lives and all around them, but they focus on the day's tragedies and travesties. That's what captures their attention, because it's what their attention looks for (whether they are consciously controlling their thoughts and attention or not).

It's possible this person believes that life is full of hard knocks and people cannot be trusted to do the right thing. To them, Life seems unpredictable and unfair. It's what they look for because it's what they believe.

Faced with situations, decisions, or problems that do not align with each other, the human mind finds some way to align them. We can either resolve them mentally or find other pieces of evidence that will support one view or another in order to create harmony. Cognitive dissonance describes a natural tendency toward mentally resolving conflict (or dissonant views) to fit our own perspective. It means that, faced with conflicting events, we resolve the conflict according to what we hold true.

The mind finds supporting evidence in the outside world to corroborate the inner belief system. Those who have negative and limiting beliefs tend to put their attention on external situations, stories, and examples that support their internal belief system. It is as if, by doing this, their mind gets to say, *See, this is the way life is*. The mind wants to achieve harmony and will find ways to create it.

Your world shows what you believe.

The thoughts of a negative thinker vibrate at a certain frequency. So do his speech and actions. In a sense, everything emanating from this person has a certain frequency, its very own energy stamp.

As this person moves through his daily activities, other things of a like nature resonate with him. As like attracts like, his own energy frequency activates similar frequencies in other people, events, and circumstances. Every negative event grabs this person's attention because its vibration matches his belief system. The belief grows stronger and stronger: *See, this really is the way life is!*

And so our dark-cloud person walks through their life being drawn to other dark clouds and amassing a collection of dark clouds. Without realizing he is doing so, he cultivates a self-perpetuating prophecy. As long as everything appears dark, he will continue to believe Life is dark. And as long as he believes Life is dark, he will continue to attract more evidence of its kind. For this person, it seems a tragedy but it's the way Life works—that whatever we believe in becomes our experience.

Your belief becomes your world.

Not only is this person operating within the confines of these beliefs, but he is also strengthening his debilitating beliefs. Sadly, most of the time, people are not aware they do this. But everyone can decide and direct the majority of their thoughts, and this is the great opportunity for all of us—to choose a more positive direction.

Let us now look at another hypothetical sort of person: the optimist.

The optimist wakes each morning and sees a bright new day. She doesn't need sunshine for the world to be illuminated and bright, because she creates her own light wherever she is. Literally and figuratively, a cloudy day does nothing to change her certainty that the sun is where it is supposed to be.

She plans her day with positive intention and a natural assumption that there is plenty of everything she needs. She believes everything will work in her favor, Life is on her side, and everyone is friendly. She approaches every person with a giving attitude and an expectation of receiving cooperation returned.

As she emanates happiness and light, it seems everything really does brighten in her path and sparkle in her wake. Others are glad to see her, and they feel good when they're with her. She says, "See, this is the way life is!" The evidence in her world supports her belief system in exactly the same way in which others' evidence supports theirs.

The optimist lives in possibilities. She does not look at the world and see the calamities that might happen; rather, she sees the possibilities of what can be. She attracts opportunities, ideas, and friends like gathering a bouquet in a field of wildflowers. Although the world might say she is in denial, in fact she skips to the beat of a different drummer, with wonderful results.

Life is to you what you believe it to be.
You experience Life according to what you
believe about Life.

Life is not limited in any way. Life is infinite and expansive. When you become aware of how you have accepted limitations into your own belief system, and how your beliefs are creating your experience, you can choose to reevaluate them, change them, and chart a new path—to a better future.

Clearly, we have all been born into situations and conditions that appear as limitations. However, there are countless examples of people who have faced daunting and seemingly insurmountable challenges and have overcome them. Some people with severe physical challenges resist giving the creative power of their thoughts over to their challenges, and instead choose to view their challenges as something to work around and through.

Dr. Stephen Hawking did not let physical disability block his ability to become one of the world's greatest theoretical physicists. Temple Grandin, severely autistic as a young girl, did not allow someone's diagnosis to become the prognosis for her life. In fact, her great success as an expert on animal husbandry came from her unique awareness of Life and her sensitivity to the lives of animals. What she accomplished was possible only *because* of her autism. What most people would see as a great limitation became the basis for her life's work, considered amazing by any standard. Dr. Hawking and Ms. Grandin are inspiring examples of the power of thought over circumstance in creating our experience of life.

It may be that your experience of life has led you to believe that Life is limited, Life withholds from you, Life judges you. Does any of this ring a bell? Have you allowed yourself to believe in limitations because of your gender, your education, your age, your ancestry, the color of your skin, or any other limited assumption? Are you willing to take a single thought or belief about yourself that doesn't feel good and change it in a way that does feel good? Consider replacing "My potential is limited because I am a woman" with a better statement, "I am unlimited *because* I am a woman," or an even better statement, "I am unlimited because of who I truly am."

Your consciousness is the sum of your thoughts, your belief system, and your accumulated awareness. It has created your life to *be*, in your experience of it, what you *think and believe* about Life.

Beliefs in the Key of Life

Your thoughts and beliefs are the rudder for the course that your life is taking. They're steering your boat. Your beliefs can hold you back, distract you from what is really so, and drain you with their limitations. Or your beliefs can empower you and support you, like using the wind to sail toward your desires.

> Beliefs have the power to create and the power to destroy. Human beings have the awesome ability to take any experience of their lives and create a meaning that disempowers them or one that can literally save their lives."
>
> —Anthony Robbins, creator of Ultimate Edge

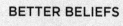

BETTER BELIEFS

Do your beliefs reflect someone who is a confident, vital partner of Life? Do your beliefs support the life you want? Do they have the potential to create the life you desire?

You are probably aware of some of your beliefs. Any statement you make about how Life works reveals your beliefs. Any statement you make about how you expect situations to pan out reveals your beliefs. Unfortunately, the beliefs you are not aware of have the same power as your conscious beliefs. And negative, defeating beliefs get the same creative spark as the positive ones.

Become aware of your beliefs to choose whether they are supporting or sabotaging what you want. The patterns of your experiences are like beacon indicators of the patterns of your thoughts. Situations that repeat over and over reveal the underlying beliefs that create and sustain those situations. Whether or not you consciously create any situations, if your response to them causes them to pan out in the same way over and over, your response reveals your beliefs.

Once you identify your limiting beliefs, you can change them. Replace every limiting belief with an empowering one. Most of the time, the opposite of a limiting belief is an empowering one. Most of the time, limiting beliefs are untruths and do not reflect the nature of Life. Empowering beliefs are truths that affirm Life's nature as your nature. Here are some examples:

LIMITING BELIEF	EMPOWERING BELIEF
I don't matter.	If I am here, there must be a purpose for me. I matter.
Nothing works for me.	Because Life requires me, Life works for me.
Others have more than I.	I am connected to Life's infinite possibilities.
That's not possible for me.	Who I am makes something perfect for me possible.
I've always been poor.	Life is abundant. Life makes everything available to me.
I'm not smart enough.	Life's infinite intelligence is mine to use.

Do these new statements feel uncomfortable or make you feel like you're lying to yourself? If it took time to establish your limiting belief, it can take time to realize the opposite as your true nature. But if you forge ahead and claim these new statements anyway, in time you will become convinced of them. Millions of people have overcome their fear of public speaking by taking a Dale Carnegie course that successfully employed the phrase "Act enthusiastic and you will be enthusiastic!"

A Foundation That Withstands Change

Your beliefs form your inner foundation. Like the foundation of a house, your foundation can be strong and sound or weak and unsteady. A weak foundation will crumble at the first appearance of something that opposes it: the unusual, unexpected, or unwanted. The slightest disturbance can knock you off your perch. However, a strong foundation will withstand anything. A shift in the wind won't knock you off your course.

You are creative, but you don't control everything that happens. Circumstances change. People change. Companies are in a constant state of change, and jobs within them change. When the economy changes, so does your bank account. People move in and out of our lives, falling in love with us, falling out of love with us, falling in love with someone else, or dying. Our tastes, interests, and intentions change, and all manner of circumstances follow suit.

If your beliefs are dependent upon conditions, then anytime conditions change (which they will), your inner foundation can shift from its base. There is nothing inherently wrong with change. Change is good, especially when it creates a better life for you. It is the nature of things to change, because Life is constantly creating.

However, no matter how external conditions change, nothing can alter what is true (and changeless) about Life.

Life's nature is changeless; love, order, peace, beauty, and abundance are eternal. Regardless of any circumstances, nothing keeps Life from expressing itself as beauty, order, harmony, and so on. Although a mountainside of trees may burn to the ground, seeds of new growth begin to sprout. In the wake of a hurricane that decimates an island, lush beauty returns quickly.

Life's qualities and activity transcend conditions and circumstances. Life's principles and truths provide a foundation that will enable you to move through life smoothly. Beliefs based on the nature of Life and how Life operates form a foundation that accommodates the changes of your life.

This new way of thinking does not mean you won't experience challenges. However, since your experience mirrors your beliefs, if your beliefs are based upon the truths of Life (e.g., peace, harmony, order, balance, flow, etc.), you can experience even the challenges as a breeze instead of a hurricane. When your beliefs align with the nature of Life, you will find it easier to respond to the circumstances affecting your life. You will be able to flow with Life instead of against it, no matter what is facing you.

Here's something to think about. At the end of each business day, the news media report whether financial markets have improved or worsened. For many people, this news influences whether they believe they're richer or poorer, all because of the conditions of the market that day. However, if you have a firm belief that Life supports you and is always working *for you*, you can respond to any market conditions from that mindset, feeling confident and powerful. If you firmly believe Life supports you richly, market changes will not keep you from experiencing your own life in rich ways. Your confidence in creating your experience *with Life's support* will generate new possibilities (i.e., ideas and opportunities) for experiencing life richly.

What if you have lost your job, your home, or your life savings because of market conditions? It might seem impossible to bring yourself to believe in Life's support when your bank account has been drained by conditions outside your control. After all, your belief does not guarantee control over other people, banks, or companies. But can you recognize the difference in responding to negative circumstances from a belief in being controlled by them, as opposed to a belief that Life is your abundant and creative partner?

Let's say that you have decided to view and respond to a life setback in a different way. How could you do that? You might ask yourself, "How can I see Life on my side in this situation?" If, for example, you lost your job, can you imagine yourself a year from now in a new job that is better suited for you? And if you can, can you look at the job you lost in a new way and see how it wasn't right for you but you just couldn't make the decision to leave?

If you've lost all your money, we can agree that it's pretty challenging to see how Life could be on your side. But are you willing to believe that Life always offers possibilities, choices, a new path?

Remember, you can't control everything, but you can control your response to any situation. You always have a choice. You can put your attention on whom to blame or perseverate on how you've been wronged. Or you can make a powerful choice of how to think, how to become receptive to new possibilities, and how to make the way for a new and better path. It's not always easy to deal with major upheavals in your life, but the important point here is that it is possible—to be willing to be willing to choose a new way.

Your belief that Life supports you will allow you to withstand anything and take a more powerful stance amid circumstances that would otherwise knock you off course. With empowered beliefs, you can *become* a new way for Life to flow with possibilities and opportunities for good. You can become a path through which Life expresses more Life.

Chapter 9

NEW THOUGHTS FOR
YOUR NEW LIFE

A Better Formula

Here's the old, classic formula for living. You may recognize it, because most of us have accepted it as the road map to success. However, while it may be an effective motivator for achievement, it often fails in helping us reach fulfillment and satisfaction.

Old formula: Have + Do = Be

When you have what you want, then you can do what you want and finally become the person you want to be. People say, "When I have enough money, I'll quit my desk job and be the artist I have always dreamed of being." "When I have accrued enough benefits, I'll be able to start my home-based business, spend more time with my kids, and be the best parent I can be." "When I retire, I'll finally take up the hobby I've wanted to do for years." "When I finally get the house/car/etc. I want, I will be living the life I dream, and I will be happy at last." "When I get rid of my debt, I can stop worrying and achieve peace of mind."

As you may have experienced personally, this model tends to keep you working toward a moving target. You never seem to get to what you really want, which is being your true self and living your dream life.

"When I *have* X, I'll be able to *do* Y and *be* Z." Does this sound familiar? Western culture is based on it. The founders of America undoubtedly thought, *When we can finally leave this taxation and oppression and start our own country, our problems will be solved forever.*

We'll use the example of money to illustrate the weakness of this formula. It's a common assumption (or creative belief) that prosperity and money are one's keys to freedom, security, and every other good experience. The belief is that money (or anything you want to have) will allow you to buy anything—the things that will ultimately secure your happiness, that is. We've all heard the common expression that money doesn't buy happiness. But if money allows you to buy everything you *want*, then why *doesn't* it buy happiness? In other words, if you have gotten some of the things you thought would lead you to happiness, why aren't you more happy as a result?

If happiness *were* dependent on money, then all wealthy people would be happy—but they're not. If happiness depended on having any particular thing, then all those who had that thing would be happy—but they're not. Similarly, if the key to happiness correlated with doing a particular thing, we'd all start doing *that*—but it's not.

Similarly, if love were dependent on being married, then all married people would be happy—but they're not. If love depended on having any thing (like a brilliant, gorgeous, diamond ring), then all those who had that thing would be happy—but they're not. If the key to love were doing something (such as dating a lot), love would be guaranteed by doing *that*—but it's not.

Happiness doesn't depend on any conditions. It depends on you being your true self and allowing Life to help you experience whatever makes you happy.

Be. Do. Have.

New formula: Be = Do + Have

This new formula allows you to *be* what's already uniquely within you and *do* what seeks unique expression through you. Life will respond to you in kind—giving you an endless stream of ideas and opportunities to express more of who you are and to do more than you ever thought possible. This brings you to the experience that what you *have* is all you ever wanted.

In this model, the creative process is set in motion by a new impetus and a new causation—your true self. Happiness isn't about the car, the money, or the anything. It's about being right now in the state of being that feeds your soul and quenches your entire experience of life.

These states of being are the qualities of Life: happiness, creativity, purposefulness, peace of mind, joy, connection, wholeness. Your true self makes the expression of these qualities unique.

You can generate any of Life's qualities because of your inseparable unity with Life. As a vital part *of* Life, you have already been given every quality that you desire. They are embedded within you.

Once you become aware of them, you can begin to feel them and start being happier.

This model eliminates the necessity to acquire or achieve anything as the only means to your dream. There's nothing wrong with acquisition and achievement, only that they are not the *only* way to happiness and fulfillment. Rather, this new model builds your awareness that you already are everything you need to be now, and expressing every part of your true nature leads the way to true happiness.

Whatever quality or state of being you desire does not depend on having or doing anything whatsoever. Feeling rich does not require money. Being an artist does not require an art degree. You can achieve either (or both) of these with what you already possess.

Being: how Life is experienced and expressed. In the absolute principle of Life, being comprises the infinite qualities of Life. Love. Beauty. Creativity. Your state of being is the way the qualities of Life become personalized and expressed by you.

Seek first the quality or state of being you most desire. From that new state, Life will respond and give to you because that is its nature. *Do* what is your nature and your intention. You will come to *have* whatever you require to live according to your true nature and your intentions.

Be. Do. Have. You are completely supported to do what your gifts and your heart impel you to do. Life will match your one-of-a-kind desires with a one-of-a-kind life. Your needs and desires are *al-*

ways being satisfied if you will raise yourself up to receive them. The Five Step Treatment explained in the next part of this book is nothing more than a technique to remind you of what is already yours.

Partner with Life

This quote is an affirmation or a mantra for many people. Written nearly one hundred years ago, by one of the greatest thinkers of humankind, it is spoken silently and aloud by thousands of people every day. It paves the way for a fresh experience.

> "My mind is a centre of Divine operation. The Divine operation is always for expansion and fuller expression, and this means the production of something beyond what has gone before, something entirely new, not included in past experience, though proceeding out of it by an orderly sequence of growth. Therefore, since the Divine cannot change its inherent nature, it must operate in the same manner in me; consequently in my own special world, of which I am the centre, it will move forward to produce new conditions, always in advance of any that have gone before."
>
> —Thomas Troward, *The Dore Lectures on Mental Science*

Imagine for a moment what might be possible for one who resolutely believes these words. Sense the power of creating a life of constant "expansion and fuller expression." How would it feel to be the center of your world, in which Life precedes you and produces new conditions *for you*? Become aware of the creative power of the universe that is right now *within you*. Realize that something greater—infinite power and possibility—is present to be awakened and activated.

Can you allow that Life is friendly and the glass is always full? When you think and live in harmony with Life, Life becomes your partner and fills your glass. Life requires you (for fulfillment of its expression and expansion) as much as you require Life (for fulfillment of your expression and expansion). It's a mutually beneficial partnership that's nothing short of Divine, and the key to creating everything you desire.

> **"There are three words that convey the secret of the art of living, the secret of all success and happiness: One With Life."**
>
> —Eckhart Tolle, *A New Earth*

Be More Now

At this point, are you reconsidering your concept of Life, that it is something greater than you, greater than this world, indeed greater than you can describe or imagine? Your willingness to think about Life in a new way will change your life.

What about your concept of yourself? Have you considered a new way of seeing yourself as a vital part of Life's expression? When you see Life's abundance, intelligence, creativity, and beauty in a landscape, have you yet realized that you are part of that landscape?

Realize that who you are already is perfect, whole, and complete exactly as you are right now. Life made no mistake with you. In fact, Life requires you. You are an important piece of the puzzle. Changing your concept of yourself is about realizing your magnificence.

Even before your toes touch the floor each morning,
you are already everything you were created to be.

Life's nature is your nature. You are a unique expression of Life. You are evidence of Life's good nature. Does this stir within you a new concept of yourself, a more expansive concept of yourself? As you welcome a new way of seeing the world, be sure to include yourself in the landscape and see yourself in a new way. Look and look and look! See more than you ever have before of who you are.

"Our deepest fear is not that we are inadequate. Our deepest fear is that we are powerful beyond measure. It is our light, not our darkness, that most frightens us. We ask ourselves, 'Who am I to be brilliant, gorgeous, talented and fabulous?'

"Actually, who are you not to be? You are a child of God. Your playing small doesn't serve the world. There's nothing enlightened about you shrinking so that other people won't feel insecure around you. We were meant to shine as children do. We were born to make manifest the glory of God that is within us. It's not just in some of us; it's in everyone. And, as we let our own light shine, we unconsciously give other people permission to do the same. As we are liberated from our own fear, our presence automatically liberates others."

—Marianne Williamson, *A Return to Love*

As you discover your true self, see how you may have allowed yourself to be less. It doesn't matter if you believed what someone else told you or you created this idea for yourself. If you choose to stop playing small and stop hiding your light, your willingness will activate powerful change. Believe differently about yourself, and Life will respond to you differently, because, according to its nature, *it must.*

This quote by Marianne Williamson was a great revelation when I first read it. Learning the process of manifesting good was so life-changing that I wanted to help others realize what was possible. But I had beliefs that held me back. For example, some of the greatest teachers overcame extraordinary odds, and their experience added to their credibility. Who was I to teach abundance if I never had to overcome poverty?

The words "Who are you not to be?" triggered a new response within me. Suddenly, I realized that my experience of abundance and prosperity actually gave me a unique perspective. Maybe I could teach abundance *because* it was second nature to me. In fact, I realized that clients and students sought my coaching *because* I could help them from my strong conviction about Life's abundance. Suddenly I had not only permission but also a passionate mission to help others create something better in their lives. It is my dream that this book inspires you to realize that you, too, are "powerful beyond measure."

....

Change who you think you are, and you may have a new experience of who you truly are.

....

Are You Ready?

You have been asked to think and believe differently to move forward in creating the change you want in your life. Are you prepared for the change you seek and more?

For many people, a welcome change would be relief from the many day-to-day challenges of modern living: relief from stress; relief from loneliness and isolation; relief from making ends meet; relief from physical problems; relief from feeling held back, put down, left out, brushed aside, forgotten, and discarded.

For others, change means things getting better than they are. Getting the right partner, the right job, the right income, the right well-being, the right acknowledgment. Getting a positive and consistent balance of health, wealth, love, and happiness.

Change can be measured on a scale divided by everything to the left or to the right of the center line, or zero. To the left of zero is a life of depletion, lack, suffering, and separation. To the right of zero is a life with plenty of everything, full of vitality and joy. Are you seeking change that moves you from negative experiences to zero, a welcome balance? Or are you seeking change that makes you feel on the positive side?

Regardless of what you are experiencing right now, and regardless of the change you desire, the change that is *possible* would blow your socks off. No matter what you imagine is possible for you, there is more. No matter what you thought Life was about, Life is more. No matter who you thought you were, *you* are more.

If you want a way out of feeling helpless, let yourself become hopeful. If you want better than the life you have now, let yourself be wooed by possibilities. And if you are willing to entertain miracles, throw open the doors!

Summary of Part II

The visible expression of your life is small compared with the infinite, invisible realm of potential. Potential energy becomes form and experience through a creative process and a receptive vehicle.

You are Life's expression, a vehicle for more Life to be expressed. Life is your partner in creating more Life. You have access to whatever you require to create whatever you desire. Using the same creative process and the same governing laws that create and sustain the universe, you can change your conditions and create the life you want.

Your experience of life reflects your beliefs about Life. Your thoughts and beliefs are powerful and creative. They set a vibrational frequency that resonates with new possibilities. Choosing your thoughts is choosing your possibilities. When you change how you see Life and how you see yourself, what you see will change before your eyes.

Your purpose is to be who you are, to cultivate the talents and dreams that are unmatched by anyone else, and in doing so to become the perfect vehicle for possibilities that are possible only by you, because of you. Life supports doing what you want and having what you want, because they are part of what is required to be you— your true self.

What's Next?

Part III describes the Five Step Treatment that you can use to daily manage your thoughts and shape your beliefs. It is designed to work with Life's nature and to affirm your connection with Life and its good.

Remember, the creative process begins with a seed, so your seed thoughts create your experience of life. The Five Step Treatment helps you plant the seeds you want for the crop you want to harvest. It changes your vibration to match what you want and allows you to realize you are co-creating it.

Part III

FIVE STEP TREATMENT

[technique • practice]

Chapter 10

THE FIVE STEPS

IN THIS SECTION OF THE BOOK, you will learn the Five Step Treatment, a technique used with great success by thousands and thousands of people. It's a tool that you can use to instantly launch yourself into better thinking and onto a path of better living. How? Well, in the same way you might see a doctor for healing, "treatment" is a remedy to heal your thinking. Just as a doctor stops a bleeding wound, "treatment" interrupts the flow of negative thoughts. As a doctor resets a broken bone, "treatment" realigns your thoughts. As a doctor prescribes helpful medication, "treatment" prescribes better thinking. Shifting your thoughts allows Life to create something new through you.

Treatment shifts your thoughts from negative ones that are creating negative circumstances to positive ones that correspond to better possibilities. It puts your attention on the good you already have, helping you to appreciate it and become confident that more is always at hand. Treatment can create an immediate realization that you already have enough (actually, more than enough) of everything you require for your best life. This new awareness launches the production of it.

Let Your Dream Be Your Guide

Your desire reveals to you something very important that is already within you. The stirring of desire is like being awakened from a deep sleep. The awakening shows you a part of your true self that is ready to be expressed by you and through you.

What if your dream is accompanied by hopelessness instead of anticipation? Hopelessness is a belief that what you want isn't possible. You can change this belief. Don't ignore your dream because you can't see how it is going to become real. Your dream shows the potential of your true self to express Life in a unique and special way.

If you don't know what your dream is, you can use Treatment to become receptive to it and to remove the mental thoughts and fears that keep you from realizing it. Everyone has desires and dreams. They call to you from deep within, as a movement of thought, as an itch, as a whisper, as an invitation from your soul. Whatever stirs your passion, makes your heart sing, and attracts you is your dream. It's as simple as paying attention to what you love, because what you love expresses your true self.

Follow what you love, what feels good. Let it be your guide.

"At first, dreams seem impossible, then improbable, and eventually inevitable."

—Christopher Reeve, actor, activist, inspirer

Consider the possibility that your dissatisfaction with your life stems from *not* expressing what makes you special. Ignoring your natural desires, gifts, and talents can build inner frustration. You're not just keeping your talent hidden; you are keeping your true self from its natural expression. A prolonged period of withholding your creative self-expression can lead to depression. Conversely, depression can dissolve when you find a creative outlet for your true nature or find ways to share your gifts with others.

"If you bring forth what is within you, what you bring forth will save you. If you do not bring forth what is within you, what you do not bring forth will destroy you."
—The Gospel of Thomas

Keeping your true self hidden from the world and from yourself not only prevents you from expressing more Life, but also depletes your experience of life. As the quote says, it'll kill you.

Nothing about you—the true you—needs to change for you to experience life more fully. You are already an amazing, unduplicated expression of Life exactly as you are. When you begin being yourself, doing what makes you happy, recognizing your true nature, and revealing your true purpose, you will begin having a better experience of life.

Follow your dream. How? Well, start believing in it, expecting it, and shaping your thoughts around it. The Five Step Treatment in this section is designed to help you do this.

Create Expectation

Life will fill the container of expectation that you provide. Life will give you a thimble full or a bucket full of whatever good you want. It all depends on your ability to accept the good that is available to you through your natural unity with Life's infinite abundance. The

Five Step Treatment will help stir your receptivity and raise your expectation.

If you want to experience more abundance, you must develop the belief that "plenty" is Life's nature and your nature, and that Life shares everything with you. Simply put, you get what you expect. Treatment will help you remove the mental doubts that keep money from flowing to you and replace them with new beliefs and expectations that Life's riches are your riches.

If you desire love, for instance, the key is to realize you are Life's conduit *for* love. You must tap into your own natural wellspring of love, give love, and watch it come back to you. No matter what you desire—love, for example—it's already within you, and now you must awaken it and let it become a magnet for more. If you want love, the Five Step Treatment can open your mind and heart to become a path for love.

The Five Step Treatment does nothing to Life. There's nothing wrong with Life; it needs no improvement whatsoever. The purpose of The Five Step Treatment is to *tune your mindset* to Life and *engage* in its natural and powerful creative process. In other words, it changes something in you that changes everything around you.

....

"You cannot solve a problem with the same consciousness that created it."
—Albert Einstein

....

Once again, you are not creating, because Life creates. Everything already exists in Life's infinite field as invisible potential waiting to be welcomed into the visible world of form and experience. Life awaits your receptivity to the good that already exists and activation to make it become visible. You are simply aligning yourself with what you desire and participating with Life's creative process to welcome it into your experience.

The Five Step Treatment helps you realize that Life is greater than you imagine, that *you* are more than you imagine, and that all you desire is already yours. In essence, this tool helps you become a vehicle for infinite possibility and creativity.

A Higher Vibration

To expect more of Life, you have to believe more about Life. To expect more for yourself, you must believe more about yourself. The Five Step Treatment will help you do this.

It doesn't matter if your desire is to relieve yourself of unwanted or negative experiences or if you want to increase the positive aspects—the process is the same. Thought precedes all form and experience. There is nothing that exists in the visible world—your own world—that did not originate in invisible thought energy. As you change your thoughts, you will experience a corresponding change in the world around you. And the Five Step Treatment is about changing your thoughts.

Of course, you'll need to take responsibility for the conditions, because some part of your thinking empowered them. You will also need to take action that supports your intentions. You cannot experience abundance if you are overspending the money in your bank account. You cannot experience more loving relationships if you are constantly judging, blaming, and otherwise separating yourself from others. You cannot find the perfect job without making some effort to uncover opportunities for it and actively putting yourself in a position to claim it. But when you begin the process of change by

BE AWARE

Notice when you come across any words or statements that meet with some resistance within
your mind or body. When you do, make a mental
note or a journal entry, and set an intention to
move on.

BE WILLING

Let your desire for change override your resistance.
Quiet your mind's tendency to resist the steps
until you have allowed yourself to change your
mindset using the steps. Remember that change
is what you seek because a new life experience is
seeking you.

changing your thoughts and following them with like actions, your
actions will have different energy and a different outcome. Treatment is a powerful means of changing your thoughts.

The Five Step Treatment will help you change your thoughts,
specifically to better thoughts with a higher vibration. It aligns your
thoughts with the nature of Life, your true nature, so that you can
experience Life's qualities and Life's power. At this higher vibration,
Life will respond to you with possibilities that match, or resonate
with, the vibration pattern of your thoughts.

Treatment will help you eliminate negative thoughts, judgment,
and limiting beliefs that are getting in the way of what you want.
When you realize you have the power to alleviate suffering by changing how you think about it, you will see your suffering from a new
perspective. At the very least, you will become hopeful that relief is

possible. At the very best, you will become confident that you can direct the course of your life.

Treatment is a way to stop thinking about being victim to outside circumstances and the actions of others. When you shift your focus to the infinite possibilities of the power that's already within you, you'll activate new ideas, opportunities, and inspiration. Victim thinking guarantees more victim experiences. Possibilities thinking leads to something new.

The Five Step Treatment is a conscious mental process to change your thoughts. It helps you cultivate your thoughts to be the perfect medium, soil, or container for your desire to manifest. It is a way to remove the resistance caused by negative thoughts and limiting beliefs. It is a way to put your attention on what you desire and become receptive to it. Turning your attention from what you don't want, toward what you do want, moves you into the higher vibration that matches and attracts your desire. This process works whether you are seeking relief from suffering, guidance out of a fog of confusion, or inspiration for a masterpiece.

"Treatment is not willing things to happen; it is to provide within ourselves an avenue through which they may happen."
—Ernest Holmes, originator of Spiritual Mind Treatment

On the following page is a diagram of the Five Step Treatment, along with a summary of each step, written as an example of a treatment. The purpose of this particular treatment is to become receptive to experiencing more good. It is written as if it is *your own* treatment; read the words aloud and see if this lifts you into an empowering mindset that is more open than before to new possibilities.

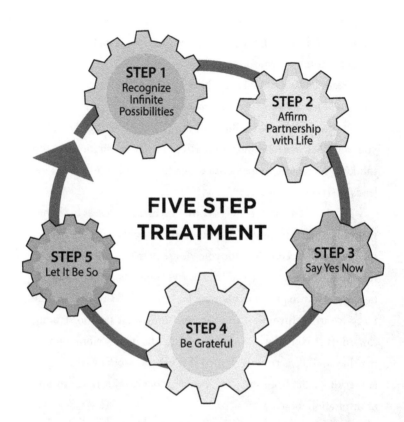

Step one: Recognize Infinite Possibilities. There is only One Life. It is infinite, abundant, and intelligent. It acts dynamically, creatively, and responsively. Life works according to orderly and harmonious law. There is no limit to its possibilities.

Step two: Affirm Partnership with Life. I am an integral part of Life. Its nature is my nature. Its power and capabilities are mine to use. I am Life's partner in creating new possibilities. Life gives me dreams and helps me manifest them.

Step three: Say Yes Now. I am already connected with all good. I say yes to new possibilities of good, yes to my better life, and yes to my truer life. Whatever I require, Life gives me and makes available to me right now. I seed my own experiences and my dreams. Life conspires with me for my own healing and fulfillment.

Step four: Be Grateful. Whatever good I name already has my name on it. I am grateful for all the good I have, all the good that is becoming, and more good than I can possibly imagine. I am grateful, too, for changing my thoughts to have this new, creative experience.

Step five: Let It Be So. Whatever Life inspires me to desire, its law creates. While I take responsibility for my thoughts, words, actions, I trust Life to create accordingly. I'm setting the sails, and Life is providing the wind. Whatever I set in motion, I release back to Life. I look forward to all the ways my good shows up.

The Science of Treatment

The process by which a seed becomes a plant is a perfect analogy for the purpose of explaining the science of treatment. Whether a seed becomes a plant or an idea becomes real, matter uses the same creative process, principles, and laws. The technique uses the principles of Life and the invisible laws (also called spiritual laws or universal laws) by which everything gets created.

"We are spiritual beings, living in a spiritual universe, governed by spiritual laws."

—Edwene Gaines, *The Four Spiritual Laws of Prosperity*

As a specific and proven method to *use* invisible spiritual laws, the Five Step Treatment provides a systematic technique to cooperate with how Life works and to partner with Life in order to co-create new form and experience.

SCIENCE

1. The observation, identification, description, experimental investigation, and theoretical explanation of phenomena.
2. Methodological activity, discipline, or study.
3. An activity regarded as requiring study and method.
4. Knowledge gained through experience.

The purpose of the Five Step Treatment is not to produce things but to produce a mindset that summons Life's creativity to bring something new into your experience. It manifests the people, circumstances, situations, experiences, and, yes, even things that match your mindset.

The Mechanics of Treatment

The five steps can be thought quietly, spoken aloud, or written. The more conviction you put into them, the more they will engage you and the greater the activation of your conviction will be. Many people who practice this technique every day prefer to find a quiet and private place so that they can speak the steps aloud. Hearing your spoken words can stir more conviction than thinking them.

Each step stands alone as a powerful declaration of truth about

Life and about you. Each step represents a principle that you can put into practice throughout your day. You may also choose to contemplate or journal about the principle in each step.

Treating for Better Conditions

A word is in order here on the subject of changing conditions. The purpose of treatment is not to change anything outside you, including conditions. You may want different conditions, and you should have what you want. You deserve whatever you desire, and Life will help you get there, but thought produces conditions, so new thoughts will create new conditions. In order to change any condition, you must change the thought pattern and the energy vibration that produced it. Hence, you are always treating to change something within yourself, and never to change something (or someone) else.

Here is a sample treatment for relieving financial strain. The goal is to shift from experiencing your life as a struggle to experiencing abundance. It is impossible for abundance and financial freedom to be created *from a mindset* of struggle and lack. Using treatment to shift to a vibration of abundance makes it possible to attract ideas and opportunities for abundance to flow.

The purpose of any Five Step Treatment is to change your mindset and perceive that what you desire *does exist, is possible, and is available to you.* If you cannot believe this, you cannot experience it. Any change in your outer world begins within you. You must change your thinking in order to believe it, see it, and experience it. Here's a treatment for this purpose.

Purpose of sample treatment: to shift my mindset from negative beliefs in lack and limitation to empowered beliefs that match

Life's nature of abundance. I want to feel the freedom of financial well-being, that Life supports me in all ways, including financially.

Step one: There is only One Life. It is everywhere. It is the source of everything. It is infinite, abundant, and intelligent. It acts dynamically, creatively, and responsively. Life flows in ways that create balance. Its possibilities are boundless.

Step two: I am a vital part of this One Life. Its nature is my nature. Therefore, if Life is abundant, so am I. Because abundance is the nature of Life, abundance is my nature. I am Life's partner in abundance.

Step three: I let go of any negative or limiting beliefs about abundance in general and money in particular. Lack is not the nature of Life, and so it is not my nature. Life does not withhold anything from me. Instead, I affirm that I am supported by Life. Everything I require is provided for me.

I expect the way to pay my bills to be revealed to me. The creative force of Life is already working for me in this way. I lift myself up to know that in the infinite field of possibilities, Life has possibilities for my support, and I now make myself receptive to them. I say yes to prosperity. I open my mind to think in new and creative ways to experience financial freedom. I open my eyes to see new opportunities.

Step four: I am grateful for my new, positive outlook about money. Life does support me in so many ways. I am grateful for all the good in my life. I am thankful for the abundance in my life now and thankful for more that is making its way to me.

Step five: Life is my partner, and I let it support me. With a new mindset that abundance is my nature, I release these words to Life's responsive nature and expect a new result that corresponds with my thoughts. I look for new conditions because I am looking from a new point of view. I am a new person, having a new experience.

Be Aware. Be Willing.

Take a moment to become aware of how this treatment felt while you were reading it silently or aloud. How do you feel now that it is over? Were the words and phrases comfortable for you to say? Did they feel empowering and inspiring? Did they lift you into a new perspective and a new, higher and lighter vibration? Do you notice any energy change in your mind or body?

Did any statements feel uncomfortable because they were different from what you have been taught to believe or from the way you have experienced the world and your life up until now? Did the words elicit negative feelings, such as shame or unworthiness? Did your mind try to put up resistance to these words with countering thoughts, such as *Who do you think you are, saying this stuff?* or *Do you really believe this is going to make anything different than the way it has always been for you?*

If this treatment elicited negative feelings, doubts, and resistance, ask yourself this question: "Am I willing to be willing?" It's possible that you have not felt part of an omnipresent Life that gives to you unconditionally. Maybe unconditional love is a foreign thought and experience. Abundance as your nature might be a new concept for you. Although the belief in abundant Life is natural and an affirmation of what's true, it is not the norm for most people.

Take a moment to recognize the reasons these words (which,

by the way, are all absolute truth) feel uncomfortable to you. Maybe they don't fit your experience (up until now), or your beliefs (up until now), or your daily vocabulary (up until now). Thoughts, words, and beliefs have created your life up until now, and new ones will create something new from this point on. However, it may take some time to create new beliefs and new vocabulary that feel comfortable and eventually even powerful.

Any discomfort and resistance might prompt some people to put this book down, never to return again. After all, you didn't buy this book to make you feel badly, so why continue? Well, you will continue because you want change in your life. You will persevere because whatever system (or lack thereof) you have used to steer your life hasn't gotten your boat to your desired destination. We all want to sail the high seas of freedom with the wind of joy in our hair. But many of us are still going in circles in the port of struggle and hopelessness. Some of us may have even left the port but can't get further than the riptide of *it never gets better than this*.

Take a deep breath. Make a choice to endure any discomfort for now (as you may have done for many days and years). It's possible you have come to a pivotal point, and if so, for now, choose to be willing.

There are several levels of willingness, ranging from total resistance to total receptivity. You will likely identify yourself on one of these levels in every situation. However, you may find that the level varies either by condition or by key areas of Life (heath, wealth, love, and happiness).

From resistant to receptive:

- Someone or something else caused this, not me.
- I didn't create it, but I can choose how to respond to it.

- If I did create it, then I can either perpetuate it or change it.
- If Life is for me, everything created offers some good for me—a gem of truth to be embraced, or a possibility to be pursued, or both.

"When you walk to the edge of all the light you have known and take that first step into the darkness of the unknown, you must believe that one of two things will happen. There will be something solid for you to stand upon or you will be taught to fly."
—Patrick Overton, *The Learning Tree*

Be willing to take the next step. Be willing to try new ways of thinking, new ways of seeing the world, and new ways of being you. Be willing for this treatment to be like a song whose beautiful notes vibrate in a way that attracts new opportunities and ideas with the same sweet vibration. Be willing for this treatment to empower you and activate within you something new and wonderful that becomes the form and experience of your new life.

Be willing to be able to create treatments every day that will change something *within* you that can change everything *around* you. Be willing to believe that Life makes possible for you whatever change you desire. Be willing to grow your willingness as your experience proves to you that treatment works. Be willing that your treatments can:

- Transform despair into hope.
- Shine light on what seems dark.
- Comfort you with companionship .
- Restore a sense of calm, peace, balance, and harmony.

- Reveal order in the appearance of chaos.
- Fill you with love, compassion, forgiveness, and understanding.
- Erase the illusory lines that separate you from yourself, from others, and from any of Life's bounty.
- Eliminate feelings of unworthiness and feelings that you are not good enough.
- Relieve blame, shame, and guilt.
- Revitalize intentions, dreams, and possibilities.
- Stimulate energy and creativity.
- Replace sickness with wholeness.
- Refresh youthful attitude and playfulness.
- Dissolve confusion with clarity, order, and light.
- Erase lines of limitation.
- Shield you from outside opinions, beliefs, and consensus.
- Remind you to always choose love.
- Abandon thoughts and beliefs that do not reflect your true nature.

Learning how to create your own treatment takes some practice. In a sense, it is an art form to cultivate. Some treatments sound like poetry, and others sound like a powerful and logical case in defense of truth. Some treatments include humor and laughter. Find a private place to shout your treatment if that's what it takes to convince your mind of new thinking. Any treatment is an effective one when it resonates with you and compels you to believe the positive and powerful words you are saying.

What is common to all treatments is that they are a unique, creative expression. A treatment affirms Life's nature and as such includes Life's qualities. Do not be intimidated by finding the right words. Just as you don't have to think of taking each breath in order for the next one to show up and support you, don't make this more difficult than necessary. Too much effort and not enough spontaneity will not affect your mind and heart in the same way as the words that come naturally to you and express themselves through you in your own unique way.

Faith and conviction are more important than the exact words you use. Faith—in Life's power and creative process, which creates everything from flowers in the field to stars in the sky to everything else in your life. Conviction—that this power and process work for you, according to their nature to do so.

The purpose of treatment is to lift you into a realization, an "aha" moment that reveals to you that you already have (and are) what you seek. It is a process of eliminating resistance and moving toward allowing the good you want. It is a way to infuse the creative energy of love into any feeling, condition, or experience in order to change it as only love can. It is a way to adjust your vibrational energy to what you desire.

Here are some additional immediate results that are possible from treatment:

- Feel lighter, as if the weight of the world has been lifted from your shoulders.
- Feel lifted into a higher realm, from hopelessness to possibilities.
- Feel lifted from a life that's mundane into a life fueled by inspiration.
- Shift from mediocrity into a partnership with genius and brilliance.
- Ignite with creativity and new ideas.

- Be receptive to thinking with Life's intelligence, loving as Life loves, and seeing through the eyes of creation.
- Feel part of something bigger than you.
- Feel in the flow, instead of left out of it.
- Find a powerful ability to direct your life and affect the well-being of others.
- Fill yourself with expectation of new possibilities.
- Be infused with the energy of something new being created.
- Be released from pain and moved into calm expectation of well-being.

Treatment establishes a new perspective that sets into motion a whole new pattern of energy and makes a whole new experience possible. Your fresh mindset entertains fresh thoughts. Your higher vibration attracts all sorts of new possibilities. You see the world through new eyes. Opportunities become apparent.

Life responds to your energy—when the energy changes within you, something changes around you.

It may not appear that your world has changed completely from this one treatment, but rest assured that it *is* changing. Sometimes change is immediate and dramatic, and sometimes it is leisurely and subtle. However, an inner shift prompts an outer response.

Pay Attention to Feelings

The Five Step Treatment changes your mindset from one of *wanting* to one of *having*. Read this again: from *wanting* to *having*. Can you feel what it's like to have the confidence that you already have everything you require for your best life, where your true self shines and is supported? Can you imagine how different your world might become as you move forward from a mindset of *having* instead of *wanting*?

Your feelings set the vibration level of your whole being. Pay attention to your feelings. Let not-good feelings guide you to change. Let good feelings point you in a better direction. Let the good feelings multiply and grow so that you are literally singing with the vibration of what you desire and what reflects your true self.

Each of the five steps has a desired thought pattern and desired feeling that you are trying to achieve. Though the purpose of your treatments will make each one unique, try to achieve some form of the desired thought and feeling. When you do, you'll have reached a new mindset and vibration that will activate new results.

Here are each of the five steps, explained in detail. In truth, each step constitutes a powerful technique of instilling better thoughts. You could spend one day contemplating and thinking about the ideas of Step One and most likely benefit from doing so. However, the Five Step Treatment combines all five steps as a proven process for deliberate and positive change. After the following discussion of each step, there will be more about the Five Step Treatment in general. In the last part of this book, you will find sample treatments for various purposes.

Chapter 11

STEP ONE: RECOGNIZE INFINITE POSSIBILITIES

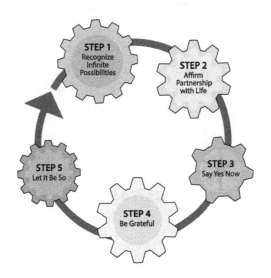

STEP ONE: **Recognize:** There is only One Life. It is everywhere, infinite, abundant, and intelligent. It is dynamic, expressive, responsive, and good. It operates according to creative, orderly and harmonious law. Life is infinite possibilities. **Create:** An expanded concept of Life. **Generate:** A feeling of awe and wonder.

Recognize Only One Life

The purpose of the first step is to direct your attention to Life (with a capital "L"). As you turn your attention to the presence and power of Life, you can begin to realize there is something greater than your desire (and includes your desire) or greater than your challenge (and includes the transformed version of your challenge).

Since treatment harnesses the power of Life for your own benefit, it is logical that you need to first recognize what Life actually is. When you stop to think about what Life really is, it's a mind-expanding experience that can make new and expansive conditions more possible.

Become aware that Life's omnipresence, omnipotence, and omniscience make it the source of everything. Recognize that there is only One Life, that there is no place (or person or condition) where Life is absent. Nothing escapes Life, including whatever it is you desire. Nothing is ever outside the purview of Life. The term "One Life" encompasses this concept.

Describe the Indescribable

Life is a single, unopposed, infinite field of invisible and visible energy—the source of everything. It is impossible to fully describe or understand Life's infinite nature. No matter what we think we know about it, scientists are always discovering more. It's impossible to wrap our human minds around the scope of it, much less to be able to fully describe it.

So let's try a simpler approach. Life creates and sustains the planets and stars and galaxies that are too numerous to be counted. There's as much Life in delicate dandelion fluff as there is in an active volcano. Life is in all the things we see and all that we cannot see. We can recognize what Life is because we are immersed in it. Everything we see and experience is Life—this much is easy, because it is obvious. What is not so obvious is all that we don't see and experience. The mystery of Life. All of that, too, is part of Life.

Not seeing something doesn't make it less real. Who would deny the reality of love, which cannot be located within the human body? Who would deny the reality of joy and peace, though they cannot be reproduced in a lab? It is important to recognize that you already know what is real without evidence of it. You already know what is true. Your resonance with Life is evidence of it. Life is real. Recognize it. Give attention to it.

Expand Your Idea of Life

Give considerable thought to what you believe about Life. Since Life responds with mathematical certainty to your beliefs, there is a direct relationship between what you believe about Life and how you experience your life. Your beliefs about Life *become* your experience.

In the step-by-step process of co-creating the experience you want, begin by surveying your fundamental beliefs that activate your experience. Do your ideas about Life support your intentions? If you want more happiness, more wealth, and more well-being, you have to believe that Life is the source of infinite happiness, wealth, and well-being.

You cannot experience what you do not believe is the nature of Life. Or, you can experience only what you believe is the nature of Life.

You cannot make lemonade out of oranges. You cannot bake a chocolate cake without chocolate. You can only get out of Life what you believe is contained in Life. Here are some examples of what this means:

If you want abundance, recognize Life's abundance. If you want love, recognize as love Life's incessant nature of giving unconditionally. If you want health and well being, recognize the inherent perfection in Life everywhere. If you desire guidance, state the ways in which Life is already infinitely intelligent and wise. If you want to get some part of your life unstuck, focus on Life's unstoppable nature to flow and move forward.

If you need proof, take a look around, because it's everywhere. You'll see overflowing abundance when you look for it. You'll see love when you look for it. If you need to see it to believe it, so be it. The purpose of Step One is to align your thoughts with what's true about Life, which is evident all around you.

The first step proclaims your understanding of Life in a way that matches your intention of cocreation. If you desire more love in your life, Step One allows you to affirm your beliefs about how love is part of Life. As you can imagine, the more you can conceive of love as a necessary, giving, flowing, and abundant expression of Life, the more it can move you toward love (as giving, flowing, and abundant) or bring love to you.

There are unlimited ways in which you can express Life. What is important is that you describe Life in ways that are meaningful to you and to your intentions. This step does nothing to Life (none of the steps do). The purpose is to turn your attention toward Life's nature as it applies to exactly what you desire now, so you can begin to see, think, and feel that Life already works the way you want your life to work.

Yeah, But . . .

Undoubtedly, your so-called rational mind is coming up with questions as to what has been stated thus far. Mental resistance will get you nowhere in manifesting what you desire. In fact, resistance blocks creative flow.

To help you lessen your resistance, common questions will be addressed in each chapter about the five steps, but they deserve further study in resources other than the ones this book provides. In fact, you should find your own way to resolve these questions with your new belief system.

Since this book is intended to simplify complicated concepts and simplify a five-step process, in the interest of simplicity, your very big and deep questions will be addressed . . . simply. The point is to help dissolve resistance and maintain your willingness to let treatment be as successful for you as it has already been for others.

Q: What if I desire something that is not Life's nature?
A: What could you want that is not some form of good? Life is only good, and your desires are for more good. To be certain, hardship, suffering, and limitation are not the nature of Life, but who would want those things? Certainly not you.

Q: If I look around and see Life's expression, I see things that are not good. I see suffering, pain, separation, and judgment. Are those the nature of Life?
A: What is natural to Life (in physical form) is whatever expresses more Life. Suffering, pain, separation, and judgment do not express more Life and do not affirm Life. The experience of any of these is very real, but its existence is not supported by the principles of Life.

Our use of the creative process allows anything to be created. We can create things we consider good and things we consider bad. We're endowed with free will that lets us create either joy or suffering. Electricity is neither good nor bad, but our use of the principles of electricity can have good results or catastrophic ones. Fortunately, for anything we experience that we don't want (pain or electrical fire), we can accept it or choose to change it and create something better.

BE AWARE
Resignation to suffering guarantees more of it. Instead, focus your thoughts on possibilities in the midst of it.

BE WILLING
Are you willing to see the doorway to something new that lies within the suffering and beyond it?

Q: What about suffering that was not created, such as being born with a debilitating disease or being caught up in the violence of war? **A:** No matter what appears, Life is not absent. Within any condition or experience, Life and its nature exist. Its inherent qualities may not be apparent, but rest assured that they are present as possibility and potential, offering a doorway to a fuller experience of Life's nature. For every kind of suffering imaginable, we have been blessed with heroes who have shown us how Life is present *in* it and greater *than* it. These heroes see light beyond the darkness and activate the potential of something different. They show us what's possible.

Affirm What Life Is and How Life Works

The qualities and activities of Life are those things that describe its nature regardless of circumstances. They exist in every expression of Life, the visible as well as the invisible, human and nonhuman, animal and mineral. For the sake of simplicity, we have already described Life as being everywhere, infinite, abundant, intelligent, dynamic, expressive, responsive, and good, but Life is also so much more—infinitely more. Here are other ways to describe Life:

Joyful.	Flowing.
Harmonious.	Expansive.
Unconditionally loving.	Serene.
Blissful.	Lively.
Peaceful.	Vibrant.
Whole.	Artistic.
Strong.	Beautiful.
Graceful.	Ingenious.
Compassionate.	Innovative.
Accepting.	Efficient.
Supportive.	Creative.
Powerful.	Perfect.
Inclusive.	Complete.
Calm.	Abundant.
Light.	Powerful.
Balanced.	Free.
Orderly.	Kind.

Feel Awe and Wonder

Step One is the starting point of realizing that Life has what you desire, and that, as an inseparable part of Life, you are already connected with whatever you desire. The bigger start you create, the more the energy vibration of your thoughts will increase. Start big, by defining Life and then expanding your concept of it, allowing yourself to feel expanded by this recognition.

The ideal feeling that you can experience as a result of this first step is one of awe and wonder. Need help feeling awe and wonder? Look at a sunrise, a sunset, a newborn baby, the crashing, powerful ocean surf, the unparalleled beauty of roses, the uncountable stars in the sky. Realize the miracle that makes these things possible. There—that's awe and wonder. This heightened feeling should already be activating a new vibration in you.

SAMPLE WORDING FOR STEP ONE

There is only One Life. It is the source of all that is. Life is intelligent, Life is creative, Life is harmonious. Life creates and gives unconditionally to what it creates.

Life continually expresses more Life by creating and by expressing more of itself through everything that is created. Life gives more Life in a continuous, flowing manner. Life is not limited in any way. It overflows with abundance.

Life is beautiful. Its beauty is in all things and in all people.

Life is perfect, whole, and complete. The essence of Life's perfection is in everything and everyone. The intelligence of Life permeates everything and everyone.

Chapter 12

STEP TWO: AFFIRM PARTNERSHIP WITH LIFE

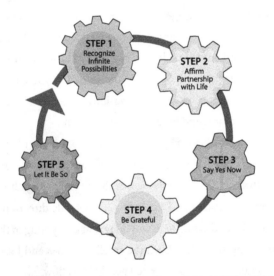

STEP TWO: Affirm: Life's nature is my nature. Life's good is available to me. Its power and creativity is mind to use. I am a vital part of Life's expression and expansion. Life provides all I require to be my true self and co-create whatever I desire. I deserve what I desire. **Create:** An awareness of unity with Life. **Generate:** A feeling of exaltation. Realizing my true nature makes more possible than I ever imagined.

In the Flow

Your words in Step One affirm what you know and believe *about Life*. Your words in Step Two affirm your union with Life and what this means *about you*.

In Step Two, recognize your inseparable connection to Life and all that Life is. Unify yourself with the nature and qualities of Life. Place yourself squarely in Life, affirming your rightful place in Life's unconditional flow. You are already part of it, but you must put your attention on this. Once again, you are not trying to change your nature but are rather focusing your *awareness* on your true nature. When you align yourself with Life, its energy becomes your energy. Its power is your power. Its good is your good. As you engage with Life's infinite power, you dissolve the illusion that circumstances, conditions, opinions, and judgments control you.

The following image may help illustrate the concept of Step Two, as well as the feelings you are trying to generate in this step. Imagine yourself sitting on a riverbank. Notice the river flowing effortlessly, the movement constant and unceasing in its single direction. There are small eddies and swirls here and there, but everything in the river is moving along smoothly. Even the small branches and leaves that have fallen into the river are carried gently in its flow.

Now you decide to put your kayak into the river. This takes a bit of effort only because the river is flowing and you (and your kayak) are not. There is a bit of temporary resistance as you cautiously manage the kayak into position. For this brief moment, you feel at odds with the river. The force of the water against the kayak moves it about as you negotiate your way into the flow.

Once you settle in the kayak, it immediately finds its bearings, going in the same direction as the flow of the river. Without any help from you or your paddle, the kayak turns effortlessly downstream and begins moving with the river. All resistance disappears, and you feel connected with the river's movement. Its direction is your direction, its energy is your energy, and its power is your power. It is effortless. Your only task is to steer this energy and this power. You point the way.

If Step One were summarized as "Life is everything," then Step Two would be "I am that, too." If Step One is about recognizing the wonder of the river of Life, Step Two is about putting yourself in it and letting yourself be carried in its current. Remember, you are a vital part of Life. Everything you desire is already part of Life and therefore available to you.

Participate with Life

Step Two affirms your connection with Life's natural and effortless flow. The truth is, you're already in it, part of it, and inseparable from it. However, you may be unaware of it, be resistant to it, or think and act against it. You can fight its power or use its power.

Resistance expends a lot of effort, which is why problems and challenges are so exhausting. Sometimes shifting from resistance to allowing is just a matter of steering in a new direction.

It is often easier to see these two extremes, resistance and allowing, in other people. Do you know someone who seems to constantly struggle and experience life as an uphill battle? Does it seem that life is harder for them and that they make it harder for themselves? At the other end of the scale, do you know someone who moves through life effortlessly? It seems that everything goes their way and falls into place at their feet.

You are an inseparable part of Life. However, you participate with Life either consciously or unconsciously, either resisting Life or flowing with it. Choosing how you participate with Life determines whether your life works for you or against you. The Five Step Treatment is about participating with Life in a way that replicates its nature in your life—expansive, intelligent, dynamic, flowing, and good.

"Allowing the truth of who you are—your spiritual self—to rule your life means you stop the struggle and learn to move with the flow of your life."
—Oprah Winfrey

Life Leaves No One Out

How often have you thought you simply aren't enough this or enough that? You may have been taught or told that you weren't given enough talent or intelligence or something along these lines. Maybe you thought you were born to the wrong family, brought up on the wrong side of town, went to the wrong schools, or hung out with the wrong people.

These ideas come from a belief that something other than you created you and doled out only certain qualities in certain measure. They imply that others got more of some qualities and that Life doesn't give to each person equally.

You may feel separate from all the wonders of Life, but you are not. You may have been told that Life's beauty is not within you, but that's just not true. What is true is that Life guarantees your connection with it and makes everything available to you.

From a single sky fall countless snowflakes, each beautiful and no two alike. They are from the same source, and yet each is unique.

In the exact same way, each of us is from the same source because there is only One Life. We cannot be separate from it. Ever.

Each of us is a unique expression of Life, with different talents and gifts that make us unique. However, our unity with Life gives us access to all of its qualities. What is true about Life is true about you. You are the expression of Life, not a separate spin-off of it.

Consider the possibility that you might have kept your gifts locked inside, where you put them a long time ago. Maybe someone squelched your creativity and you never even tried to be an artist, an actor, or a dancer. Maybe your beliefs about yourself squeezed the life out of the amazing talents hidden within you.

Artists get inspired to create art. Teachers get ideas about how to educate others. Life makes possibilities available all the time, but we can receive them only according to our beliefs about who and what we are. While you may not become a professional athlete simply by believing you are one, studies have proven the power of thought to improve physical performance. It's your life experiment. Give yourself permission to express your true self, regardless of what anyone may have said about you or convinced you to believe about yourself. See what happens.

As an expression of Life itself, you cannot seriously think you are not enough of . . . well, anything, actually. Certainly, if you've always believed you're not enough, it might take a bit of time to believe otherwise. However, there is nothing more important than changing your mindset to embrace—and ultimately celebrate—who you are. Use the Five Step Treatment to shift your mindset to realize your value and significance.

Expand Your Idea of You

Your *true* nature encompasses your unity with Life's nature, as well as your uniqueness. What is *unique* about you? What are the gifts that are yours alone to cultivate and express? What might you bring from possibilities into realities that no one else can? What is given new expression because of you? What might not be possible in the world without you?

Your true self is a unique expression of Life. You are Life's emissary. Your true purpose is a catalyst for Life's impulsion to express more Life. You are vital to Life and therefore to the entire world. Without you, something—no, make that everything—would be different.

Don't stop there. Keep elevating your sense of self. You *can't* be too big for your britches. You are an unrepeatable miracle. You are a divine creation and here by divine appointment. You are co-creator and co-partner with a power that stirs the currents of the ocean.

"I am secure, for I know who I am: a richly endowed child of God. I am secure in all I do, for I know my oneness with the divine process. I am secure in all I have, for I know my treasure is in my mind, not in my things. I live my Life from day to day as if God's supportive substance were as exhaustless and dependable as the air I breathe, which it most certainly is."

—Eric Butterworth, *Spiritual Economics*

Feel Exalted

If you have gotten yourself to an understanding that you are the beloved of the universe, you should be feeling pretty special indeed. You *are* special. (Everyone is special; no one is superior to another.) You are imperative to Life. You are how Life shows up in the world and how Life is expressed.

The goal of this step is to really believe these words and to get to the feeling of exaltation. Not false exaltation, but true amazement at your significance and your unity with Life. The energy of this feeling will lift your vibration to a higher level and will activate new possibilities.

One who realizes their value will have a different (and better) experience of life than one who does not believe they have any value. Remember the words of Thomas Troward, "My mind is a centre of Divine operation"? You are the center of your world, and your world is important.

....

"You are not who you think you are. You are not an ordinary human being living in an ordinary world. You are an astonishment of capacities, and you are here to reach your highest potential."

—Tama Kieves, *Inspired & Unstoppable*

....

Yeah, But . . .

Q: I can say these words, but deep inside, I don't believe them. How can I feel exaltation when I truly feel small?

A: Fake it until you can believe it. If you consistently and persistently affirm your specialness and magnificence, eventually you *will* believe it. These praising words will seep into your subconscious and slowly become your mindset. (After all, isn't that how you came to believe otherwise?) The Five Step Treatment can improve your perception about yourself. Be willing to love yourself as Life loves you.

TRUE SELF

Whom do you admire in the world? What qualities do you admire in them? Do these qualities touch something within you? Is it possible these qualities resonate with you because they are the qualities your true self yearns to express?

Can you find examples of people who have helped the world by letting their true selves shine? Whom do you know personally who celebrates who they are? Does their being their true self rob you of anything at all, or does it lift you because of their presence and example?

Q: Will my wanting more mean there is less for others?

A: This is about your *being* more, not *wanting* more. More wanting will create more wanting. Your purpose is to express more Life. More being will create more Life, which is the purpose of Life and your purpose as an expression of Life. Being more will allow you to help others in so many more ways than being small does. When you desire more and dream more, you will be able to help and serve more. As a conduit to expressing more and more Life, you will enable others to benefit. And when you focus on being more of who you already are, you will find that more of what you truly want to have and do will find their way to your new and expanded way of being. In other words, being true to yourself will ultimately manifest things you love to do and have.

Q: How can I not feel selfish and guilty about my dreams and desires, when others suffer?

A: When you understand the interconnectedness of all Life, you will understand that your purpose of realizing your dream *will* ultimately benefit others. Living your best life lets you fill a spot in the world that is yours to fill. You are doing your part. Not only are you an example to others (regardless of whether it is apparent), but some part of your purpose also serves others. Doing without and being less serves no one.

> "If you are not selfish enough to be in alignment with Source energy, you have nothing to give (to the world)."
>
> —Esther Hicks, author of *The Law of Attraction*

SAMPLE WORDING FOR STEP TWO

Anything that is true about Life is true about me. I am Life's expression and Life's inlet and outlet of creativity. What Life is, I am.

Life breathes through me. My breath is evidence of my unity with Life. That which makes it possible for me to breathe has no limits, and neither do I.

I am as much a part of the beautiful landscape as a single blade of grass and a mighty oak. Like the blade of grass, Life provides everything I need to live abundantly and vibrantly.

Life shows up through me and as me. Where Life is, I am. And where I am, Life is. There is no separation between Life and me. I am one with Life. I am Life. I am vital to Life.

(continued on next page)

(continued from previous page)

The presence and power of Life is within me and around me. I am evidence of Life's infinite creativity.

Like a drop in the ocean that contains every property of the ocean, all of Life is within me.

I know that the intelligence of God that orchestrates the galaxies and paints a beautiful sunset each evening is the same intelligence that informs every cell in my body.

Life is loving and giving, and so am I. Love fills me and radiates from me.

Chapter 13

STEP THREE: SAY YES NOW

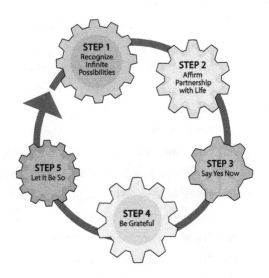

STEP THREE: Yes: I claim my partnership with Life. I accept that Life works with me, through me, for me and because of me. My thoughts are creative and powerful. I choose to express my true self, realize my dream, and live my best life, my way. **Create:** Positive and empowered declaration that all is well, right now. **Generate:** A feeling of fulfillment as a result of shifting from wanting to having and receiving.

Pull Weeds. Plant Seeds.

As in nature, when you plant the seed of new thoughts, what grows is new form and experience that matches the seed. What you plant is what you get. Acorns produce oak trees. Orange seeds produce orange trees. Poverty thoughts produce poverty. Loving thoughts produce loving experiences.

Step Three provides the opportunity to plant new seeds. Their sprouts comprise ideas, opportunities, and a new path of experience. However, usually before any seeds can be cultivated to burst forth in full glory, some weeding is required.

Worry and doubt are like weeds that choke sprouting possibilities and stifle creativity. Old fears and negative thought patterns can rise to the surface and spread quickly if left unchecked. Further, fear, worry, and doubt can lower your vibration and counteract all the great work you may have invested in your new mindset. You cannot generate the vibration of what you do want when you focus on, and generate the vibration of, what you don't want.

Use the Five Step Treatment to eliminate fears and banish worry. Before you claim what you desire, you must first strip your fears of the power you've allowed them. Steps One and Two establish the foundation to do this. Declaring your inseparable connection with Life enables you to deny the negative thoughts that contradict these truths and principles. In other words, acknowledging the power in what's true makes it that much easier to remove the power from un-true, manufactured thought.

When you experience excessive worry, use the Five Step Treat-ment to make an airtight argument for yourself about the futility of negative thinking. Remind yourself that lack or limitation is not Life's nature and it's not your nature, either. Remind yourself that Life supports you and is always for you. Remove the power you may have given your worries and fears. Boldly affirm that they have no principle that supports them. Show your negative thoughts the exit door.

Be firm in letting go of limiting thoughts and beliefs. However, be careful not to spend too much time in your denial and speaking ill of them, because you don't want to tune your vibration to them. Get rid of them and move on to align yourself with what you do want, so your energy attracts it.

> "Good and more good is mine. An ever-increasing good is mine. There is no limit to the good which is mine. Everywhere I go I see this good, I feel it, I experience it. It presses itself against me, flows through me, expresses itself in me and multiplies itself around me."
>
> —Emma Curtis Hopkins, pioneer of the New Thought movement

Out with the Old. In with the New.

The purpose of Step Three is to create a shift in your mindset to shed old thoughts and beliefs and replace them with new beliefs aligned with your desires (and the principles that make them possible). This vibrational shift within you reverberates beyond you and brings about new forms and experience.

New form can appear in infinite ways—gifts, checks, tickets, houses, cars, school acceptance letters, job offers, and so on. New experiences are also boundless—ideas, inspiration, revelations, feelings of lightness and expectation, renewed energy, increased resolve, new perspective, youthfulness, improved health, playfulness, dissolved resentment, unleashed creativity, rekindled love, and so on.

Here is an image you can use to activate a shift in your mindset. Imagine that the current state of your life is a painting on the wall. This painting is a reflection of the thoughts and beliefs that you have created. It is the picture of your current life that you want to change.

As you begin Step Three, describe the things in the painting that you want to remove from your life. In essence, you are releasing the old, outdated, and unwanted. Categorically deny the necessity of anything negative. Remind yourself that anything in your life picture that is not supported by Life's nature, Life's principles, and your grand dream has no place in your life now.

In your mind, remove the old picture and remove unwanted thoughts and beliefs in your words. You can say things like, "I no longer believe I am limited in what I can do, because nothing limits Life and I am Life's expression." Or, "Lack has no business in my life, because it is not supported by Life. I let go of any thoughts and beliefs in lack now."

Once you feel you have removed the old image, immediately create a better one. In fact, replace the old with the opposite and use an affirmation to do this. For example, if you said, "I let go of all limitation," directly follow this statement with an affirmation, such as, "I am an expression of Life that is limitless. There are no boundaries on who I am and what I can do." Describe the new picture of your life in words that claim the nature of Life as your nature. Affirm your good with confidence. Paint the fullest picture of your new life until you are satisfied that the picture expresses your desires and you get excited that the picture is activating new possibilities.

If it helps you to accept your good by describing the actions and results that create the fulfillment you desire, do so. However, do this in a way that does not overly define or limit Life from revealing other possibilities that will satisfy you in ways you haven't thought of. You can say, "I accept my new home being revealed as I look for it . . . or something better." As in every step and in all of your words, remember that you are not influencing Life; you are influencing only your own thoughts and the vibration you put out into the world. Life will produce according to your thoughts and wishes or will deliver something you didn't expect, which will be at least as good as, if not better than, what you imagined.

From Wanting to Receiving

We often state our desires in terms of wants or needs. We often dream of what we want in terms of when they happen someday. Unfortunately, wanting and needing separate you from what you want. As long as you continue to have the mindset of need or want, you hold your desire beyond your reach. In other words, wanting creates more wanting, not having.

Let's return to the example of putting your kayak into the river. Waiting for the river to take you and your kayak along its merry way "someday" will leave you stranded on the bank until it gets dark, you lose interest or get discouraged, or all of the above. You'll stomp away, dragging your heavy kayak, and disown your "someday" desire as if it were a soggy sweatshirt. Meanwhile, all you really had to do was put the kayak, and yourself, into the river and be taken along with it.

Did you know scientists have proven that our brains cannot differentiate a real experience from an imagined one? To the brain, if we see it and imagine it, it is as real as if we really experience it in form. Therefore, as we refine what it is that we desire, we begin its creation and its reality—in our brain. In Step Three, state your desires as already existing now. You have created them as an idea in your mind's

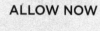

ALLOW NOW

Nothing in your life has to change in order for you to feel freedom, love, connection, joy, balance, abundance, or any aspect of good. If you allow it now, you can experience it now.

Skepticism and doubt create resistance that keeps you from the good you seek. Allow yourself to feel the quality you want, because your vibration will activate its manifestation.

eye. You see it, you feel it. It is real to you. In fact, your statements are in the present tense, because that is exactly where your good is.

Right now, you can achieve the feelings and qualities you want, without any circumstance having to change. If it's wealth you desire, get the feeling of it now, get excited about receiving it, and get the feeling of having it. The vibration of your expectation can generate ideas and opportunities.

Whatever you desire, let go of needing or wanting it and shift into the energy of receiving it. Let the creative process match your new vibration with a new and corresponding experience or form. This is about changing your *mindset* from needing and wanting to accepting and expecting in order to set into motion a change in the facts of your life.

This is how everything that is in form is manifested. Everything begins as an idea. Everything that becomes yours starts as an idea, a thought, and the picture you create in your mind. Once it is real in your mind, on the inside, your picture can become real on the outside, too.

"We tend to get what we expect."

—Norman Vincent Peale, *The Power of Positive Thinking*

The Benefits of Partnership

The river is your partner, but it can't help you if you remain sitting on the riverbank. You have to take a step toward it and accept your place in it so it can carry you in its powerful flow.

As you begin to accept and expect what you want, you are doing your part in partnership with Life. You are stepping *up to* Life. You are putting yourself squarely in its vortex of power and possibilities.

You don't have to wait for Life to come to you, because it's already right where you are. Everything that is Life's is available to you. You can choose to become its partner and accept its good and its infinite possibilities. Whatever you desire is not on the far bank of "someday" but is where you (and your kayak) are right now. Let yourself be carried by the flow that turns your ideas and inspirations into real things and experiences.

The law of cause and effect states that every effect results from a corresponding cause. We tend to think that there is first a cause and then an effect, assuming a sequence that implies a lag of time in the process of manifestation. Actually, according to quantum physics, both cause and effect exist simultaneously, because in the realm of the absolute (where time and space do not exist, since they are concepts of humankind), everything exists simultaneously. Questions and answers exist together. Problems and solutions exist together.

Right now, you are connected to everything. Nothing is separate or distant from you. Your next brilliant idea isn't far away at all. The solution to every problem isn't merely available; it's available right now. Your dream is already right here, right now.

The Power of Now

Consider this moment right now. In this moment, the past is already over and the future hasn't happened. In fact, this moment was the future . . . a second ago. This is important, because every now moment is rich with creativity that is creating your future.

Creativity does not happen in the past or in the future. You cannot create something to happen yesterday, last year, or a century ago. And the future is merely an imagined possibility until you arrive at it, when it is no longer the future but the present.

In this now moment, you can make a fresh choice, choose a new response, and lay a new path for something different than what you've experienced so far. This now moment is rich with possibility.

> "The quality of your consciousness at this moment is what shapes the future—which, of course, can only be experienced as the Now."
>
> —Eckhart Tolle, *The Power of Now*

Your present thoughts are creating your current reality and establishing your future. Your ideas and imagination are activating a creative process that is happening in this very moment. Though the air around you seems invisible and unmoving, there are countless unseen miracles happening right this second.

Right now, an unseen force is holding you on this planet as it speeds through seemingly empty space. The forces of gravity, electricity, and thermodynamics, and all sorts of laws of physics, are happening, whether or not you see or even feel them. In fact, within your body, literally millions of things are happening simply to sustain your circulation, balance your internal systems, and provide your next breath. In the same space, at the same time, unseen forces and laws are responding to the energy vibration of your thoughts, ideas, and desires.

Seize this creative present moment and accept what you desire—right now. See it from the perspective of *having* instead of *wanting*. As you become one who *has*, that pattern vibration attracts to you forms and experiences that match your satisfaction. Dreaming about a better future is worthwhile if it redirects your attention from what you don't want or don't have toward what you do want and so greatly desire. However, creating is a now experience.

Stop worrying about a past you cannot change or hoping for a better future. Invest this present moment in a scientific, creative process that creates everything. Here is your opportunity to plant the seed of your intention and expect what you plant to bear fruit. Every moment contains the seed—and its fulfillment.

Feel Fulfilled

Does claiming your desire as already yours bring you a sigh of relief or a sense of great fulfillment? In this step, the acceptance of your desires may be accompanied by a sense of fulfillment, as if there is nothing more to do. In a sense, there *is* nothing more to do but to see everything from the new viewpoint of *having* instead of *needing* or *wanting*.

When you're certain that Life is for you, you stop focusing on what's missing from your life—because you're too busy gathering evidence of what you're co-creating with Life.

Fulfillment builds your anticipation that something wonderful is in the process of creation right now. After all, one who *has* is supported completely by Life. From the infinite field of possibilities, you attract new forms and experiences that match your expectations. Life provides new opportunities, ideas, circumstances, and happy surprises.

What if you can't get to a feeling of fulfillment? Maybe years of disappointment have resulted in doubt and uncertainty, and that makes fulfillment seem impossible. Maybe you're (still) uncertain about the nature of Life and your nature. If so, don't judge yourself harshly. Feeling badly about not being able to summon fulfillment only creates more negative energy. Judgment, blame, and shame are part of a downward spiral that creates more judgment, blame, and shame and lowers your vibration further than before.

Let's nip this in the bud to keep you from undoing your good work and help you move in the right direction. Here are a couple of ways *toward* fulfillment.

You might be leaping further ahead in your dreams than your mindset is ready to accept. You deserve anything you dream, but you might not believe it yet. Shift your mindset to something you *can* accept completely.

If you can't even pay your bills today, it could be impossible to achieve a feeling of true financial freedom. However, can you feel what it would feel like to pay all the bills you owe today? Can you feel *that* fulfillment? If you can remember a time when you did have this feeling, can you allow the memory to create the feeling within you now?

No matter what you desire, there is a feeling that corresponds to it. Fulfillment is a feeling that goes along with being, doing, and having what you want. Get that feeling now with whatever technique works. Small steps in this process will help you experience greater and greater acceptance of the good you desire. With each step, give yourself permission to feel fulfilled.

Many new students of this process undertake a desire for millions of dollars or a complete reversal of disease. It is definitely possible to achieve both with this process, and many, many people have done so. However, if you can't accept that what you want is possible and you can't feel its fulfillment, you can't make the best use of this creative process. Few people can immediately shift their mindset to fully accept, without doubt, instant and complete physical healing.

Remember you cannot experience what you do not believe. Start with something you *can* believe in. Start by building the belief that Life's constant flow supports you in paying your current bills, if you can accept that. Start by building the belief that Life's intelligence is working right now to strengthen your body and guide your doctors, if that's what you can accept.

Here's Roger's story. Receiving a diagnosis of prostrate cancer, he considered how to use these principles to co-create his own healing. He didn't truly believe he could heal his cancer by himself. But he had an idea (because he was receptive to an idea from the limitless source of infinite intelligence) of what he *could co-create*.

Roger believed he could visualize his cancer changing from a nebulous, sprawling mass into a distinct and concentrated unit, completely surrounded by healthy cells. Instead of healing the cancer himself, he thought he could at least use his thoughts in a way that would help his doctors remove the cancer.

Every day leading up to his surgery, Roger dedicated time to seeing his desire as already done, to seeing a distinct mass that could be removed easily. He did Five Step Treatments for this purpose: to shift his mindset to accept this new possibility.

The surgery was successful, and the doctor proclaimed Roger cancer-free. When the doctor showed Roger the pathology report that was prepared prior to surgery, it described the cancer as completely localized in one spot, completely surrounded by healthy cells—exactly as Roger envisioned and accepted in his Five Step Treatments.

Find the point where you can believe what you desire, and feel its fulfillment. Use the sample Five Step Treatments in Part IV to help you build a new belief, move up the spiral of your own growth, and raise your vibration to a new possibility you can fully accept. Fulfillment happens when you realize that what was once only a possibility is right now becoming your new reality.

Yeah, But . . .

Q: Just saying I have what I desire gets me my desire? This seems too simple.

A: It *is* simple. Notice others who move through life effortlessly. A parking spot appears just as they need it. They receive a phone call from a prospective client after they have stated their desire for new business. Pay attention to what they believe, what they expect, what they say, and how they act. Observe all the ways in which they work with Life instead of against it. Notice the flow and the lack of resistance in their thoughts, words, and actions. Can you recall instances when you experienced this?

It *is* simple, but it takes practice and consistency. It may be easy to state your desire, but keeping your thoughts positive can be a full-time proposition. Many of us must constantly weed the garden of our minds in order to cultivate the seeds of possibilities so that they may grow and thrive. As you change the pattern of your thoughts and consciously replace limiting beliefs with empowering ones, you'll find it easier to keep your thoughts on track.

Here's an experience of my own process. My husband and I were traveling down a highway in our separate vehicles, when I noticed the license plate fall off his car. As soon as I was able to signal to him, we exited the highway and pulled off the road to decide what to do next. We had already driven pretty far from the spot where the plate would be, but it was important to retrieve it. I should explain that my husband's car is an antique car (given to him by his grandmother) and the license plate was its original.

I immediately did a Five Step Treatment aloud for both of us. My purpose was to stem the onslaught of negative thoughts about the impossibility of finding the license plate, the dangers of a busy highway, and on and on. Instead, I wanted to remind us that we live in a universe that is orderly, that works for us, and in which nothing is ever lost.

After a few circling attempts, we located the plate—lying at the guardrail, across three very busy lanes of traffic. As we wondered how we could retrieve it safely, a highway worker suddenly showed up. Without hesitation, he offered to get it and bring it back to us. Was this mere coincidence or Life helping us? Does it matter? My experience matched my belief (that Life works for me when I work with Life) and made my belief stronger.

It *can be* simple. The key is to make the choice to *use* the creative process. In this example, we chose to adjust our own thinking first and let a new experience follow. Sure, we could have retrieved the license plate ourselves. We could have waited for a break in the traffic to go get it (we'd probably still be waiting). We could have experienced the stress of running across a major freeway. We could have been hurt.

Instead, we chose to let Life offer a better way. We chose to believe Life helped us. We chose to call it a miracle and to allow more to follow.

It *is* simple, but it takes effort and commitment to use all the tools in this book. However, the rewards of doing so are infinite: small ones, like receiving help on the highway, to big ones, like getting a breakthrough idea or finding the love of your life around the next corner.

Q: How can I claim and accept something that isn't what I see in my life?

A: Do not be fooled by appearances. This whole process is about giving the power of your thoughts to infinite, invisible energy and Life's natural creative process. Everything you see (form and experience) is the *effect* of thought, not its *cause*. What you see is constantly changing, and you are directing its change. As you synchronize your thoughts, beliefs, and actions with Life's abundant nature, you'll get new thoughts and new ideas. These will lead to the creation of new, abundant conditions. Believe creativity is happening, look for it *from* a sense of certainty in it, and you *will* see it. Look for miracles, and that's what you'll find and create more of.

Q: What if what's in my life now isn't even close to what I want?

A: The same creative process creates everything. Don't waste time trying to figure out how you might have created something you don't want (unless it helps you to identify patterns that prevent or limit your belief in change). In Roger's story, he didn't dwell on the cause of his cancer; he turned to the creative process and his partnership (with Life and with his doctors) for new possibilities in healing.

No matter what's in your life now, the only way to change it is to think differently about it. What if you're facing bankruptcy and that seems completely in opposition to the financial freedom you want? How can you shift your thoughts toward freedom? Maybe you can believe bankruptcy offers you a fresh start, a slate wiped clean of unbearable debt. Maybe this fresh start makes you receptive to new ideas and new choices. Can you see how this shift might put you on a path toward freedom? See everything as evidence of Life's good nature.

Whatever the state of your life now, you can choose to look at it in an entirely new way: "Well, this *is* in my life, and if Life is *for* me, then there must be something in this *for* my good. Either I can find out the good (or the potential) in it now or I can be willing to understand it at some point when I am more ready to appreciate it." Make a choice to shine a new light on whatever exists so you can see it in a new way and experience it in a new way. Be willing to be willing.

"Life will give you whatever experience is most helpful for the evolution of your consciousness. How do you know this is the experience you need? Because this is the experience you are having at this moment."

—Eckhart Tolle

Q: I'm still skeptical. I can claim whatever I want and get it?
A: Let's do a quick review. Happiness isn't about getting anything outside you (things, fame, fortune). If outside things determined your happiness, then when those things changed or went away, so would your happiness. And if this were true, then everyone with "things" would be happy (and you know this isn't always the case).

True, lasting happiness comes from within. It comes from feeling connected to the unending flow of the qualities of Life that fill your heart and support your true self.

Anything you want (home ownership, a great job, a loving partner) has a quality in it that points to what your heart yearns for. Love. Acceptance. Peace. Joy. Harmony. Set your sights on experiencing the quality you want above all else. It is available to you right now, and if you can feel even a bit of it, you can realize there is even more available.

The Be-Do-Have model focuses on feeling the contentment of expressing your true nature first and allowing all else to fall into place. Once you begin experiencing any state of being you choose, you can be receptive to the forms and experiences that match it. Allow Life to give you some new and better way to experience the quality that you imagined.

SAMPLE WORDING FOR STEP THREE

I eliminate all false, limiting, and disempowering beliefs from my mind that are in the way of my fulfillment.

I allow new thoughts that are empowering and Life-affirming. These new thoughts create patterns of belief that build my new foundation of faith brick by brick, a powerful base for wonderful creativity.

My perfect, right work is effortless, easy, fun, exhilarating, creative, and rewarding. I have the freedom to create and the freedom to do whatever I want. I have plenty of good to share. I am rewarded with treasures, rich beyond compare.

The path to my highest good lays itself before each step I take. The atoms of the universe rearrange themselves to present the highest good and perfect opportunities to me every single day. Each day, I am intuitively drawn to have thoughts and take actions that harmonize with what makes me happy.

Everything in my life works perfectly. Everything I touch turns to gold. Fragrance precedes me. A halo surrounds me. Pixie dust trails me. Doors open to me. Obstacles melt away around me. Money flows to me with ease and overflowing plenty. Clarity and intuition guide me. Giving generously humbles and thrills me.

I am an example of good living. I am a drop in the ocean that creates waves around the world. My good life is an essential drop that makes the cup of peace overflow its brim around the world.

I know without doubt that Life is where I am— in my body, in my mind, in the medical and nursing staff caring for me, and in the surgeons restoring me. Every wise action by my doctors is guided by Life's infinite intelligence to reveal my greatest and most magnificent health. Everywhere is evidence that Life is with me and for me. Life's healing light transforms everything unlike it and reveals my rightful wholeness and perfect health. This experience has served its purpose, and now in its place is a new purpose, a new invitation for me to experience Life's perfect presence within me.

My own existence proves that I am loved by Life. My specialness and uniqueness make me lovable. As I celebrate the gift that I am, others are irresistibly drawn to my energy. From this sea of people, I get to choose the mate who is perfect for me. Life is not limited in possibilities, and neither am I. My perfect partner already exists. As I feel the love I desire, I expect Life to bring me experiences and a loving partner that match this love.

Chapter 14

STEP FOUR: BE GRATEFUL

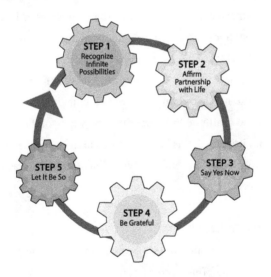

STEP FOUR: Appreciate: My better thoughts are creating better results. Grateful for the shift in my mindset that sets a new cause toward a new effect and allows more good to flow. I celebrate my participation with Life. **Create:** Uplifted vibration of gratitude from a new, positive outlook. **Generate:** A sense of completion.

Be There Now

You have partnered *with* Life; you have seen how Life works with you when you work with it. You have put your kayak into the river, and it's taking you to your dream. You have experienced the ease and flow of being in nonresistance and in the creativity of Life.

No longer the victim or puppet of others or of forces you do not understand, you are now among those who understand how Life works and how to work with Life. How does it feel to live your life in the direction in which Life flows, instead of against it? How does it feel to be master of your ship, with the wind as your benevolent partner? How does it feel to know that you are important to Life? How does it feel to know that Life is on your side?

Step Four lets you put into words the relief and the joy of realizing that you are co-creating your own life, *with* Life. You express happiness and gratitude to be experiencing what you have dreamed and felt and imagined. It is here now! Proclaim your relief, your celebration, your gratitude, and your fulfillment. In doing so, you will cultivate more.

Gratitude Lifts You

Gratitude changes your energy vibration, lifting you up *to* a greater experience of Life. The moment you align *with* Life, you begin to vibrate at a higher frequency, matching the frequency of Life. At this higher place, all the qualities of Life vibrate on the same wavelength—love, joy, happiness, harmony, peace, and so on.

Gratitude lifts you up to the pivotal point where possibility and reality abide together.

Life does not bow down to us, nor would we want it to. In truth, we are part of Life, never actually above or below it. But we want to lift ourselves up to the high vibrational level of Life because that is where perfection, harmony, and beauty are. That's where we want to be!

Like a beacon of light, gratitude dispels the darkness. In this fourth step, you might notice that resistance of any kind—especially to the good you so desire—has been dissolved or eliminated. Without resistance, you can move into the creative state of allowing. It is impossible to feel anger, resentment, or fear when your focus is being thankful. Any feelings that oppose gratitude cannot exist when gratitude is present. In fact, gratitude also shifts your attention away from a sense of *need* and toward feeling satisfied with all that you *have*.

Notice throughout this book that the word "need" is rarely used. Instead, the words "desire" or "require" are used, because they convey a greater sense of power and possibility. Thoughts of need generate more experiences of need. See the difference?

Gratitude is a practice of awareness that expands your receptivity to good. Gratitude raises our awareness of Life's abundance as our abundance. When we're grateful, we love what we have and can become receptive to experiencing more of Life's bounty.

Better Equation = Better Results

When you accept what you desire as yours and feel fulfilled, *you* become a new equation for Life's law of creativity. Let us consider some old equations of being in light of this new equation.

Old equation: Life is limited + I don't have enough = Life never gives me enough.

New equation: Life's bounty is mine + Grateful for what is mine = I always have plenty to be grateful for.

Old equation: Life is lacking + I am not good enough = Life doesn't support me.

New equation: I am Life's beloved + I am perfect exactly as I am right now = Life supports me because Life is me (and I am grateful).

The new equations make more of Life's good available to you because you make yourself more available to Life. Every step in the Five Step Treatment is designed to align your vibration *with* Life and to allow you to remain at that high vibration of possibilities.

Gratitude Multiplies Good

Whatever you put your attention on expands and multiplies.

Genuine feelings of gratitude send out waves that return to you more to be grateful for. Suddenly, opportunities, phone calls, offers, and all kinds of possibilities make their way to you, brought by the thankful vibration generated *from* you and Life's responsiveness *to* you. Suddenly, there's more to be grateful for, which will attract even more.

Yeah, But . . .

Q: How can I feel grateful, when I cannot forget about what's happened to me?

A: Regardless of what has happened in the past, this moment is ripe with creativity for a new possibility. Carrying blame, shame, regret, and resentment supplies negative energy to Life's creativity, generating more of exactly what you *don't* want. Gratitude shifts your attention to all that you have and all that is good. It does not deny your past but rather helps you move beyond it into a new future.

Q: What if being constantly grateful, happy, and fulfilled creates a big contrast to the usual mode of my family (or friends, or culture, or religions, or spouse, or . . .)?

A: Gratitude is a natural response to being in the flow of good. Gratitude, happiness, and fulfillment honor Life as the source of *all good* for all people. Radiating these qualities distributes them beyond your own experience to the people around you and the world at large. You become the example, the teacher, the invitation, and the permission that others need to welcome their own happiness and fulfillment. Trust Life working through you, for you, and for all. You're a blessing to everyone when you become a higher possibility yourself.

Feel a Sense of Completion

Completion is the feeling you get from a job well done. At this step in treatment, you've done a great job of shifting your thought and vibration. Aligning your thoughts with the infinite power and possibilities of Life is an accomplishment. It feels like the easy-flowing energy of the river because it duplicates the nature of Life, carrying you in its graceful flow.

Gratitude and completion fill us, uplift us, and expand us. Like the river, gratitude carries us in the direction *of* Life.

When you know you have shifted your thoughts, you can be assured something new is being created to match them. You are receptive to wonderful new possibilities. You become a funnel for the infinite to flow into your life and pour into the lives of others. Life's abundance finds easy, welcoming, and fertile expression through you.

SAMPLE WORDING FOR STEP FOUR

I am grateful for my new mindset that aligns on the side of Life.

I am grateful for the good that I have, the good that is becoming, and the good that I have yet to imagine.

I give thanks for my willingness to create change and my expectation of change.

I am grateful for my new appreciation of who I am and how I am co-creating more for myself and others.

My heart overflows with love as I see my life through new eyes, realizing all the blessings, all the ways others make my life good, all the ways I can give and serve from an infinite flow of good.

I am thankful for the realization of my highest good and that my nature is Life's nature. I am thankful for the source of all that is. I am thankful for my new mindset in realizing that there is only One Life which makes all available to me right now.

In advance of the demonstrations of this treatment, I give thanks because I know and believe that Life is already working for me and for my highest good.

For this thing or experience I treated for, or for something better, I am grateful. I already have the quality I am seeking, as well as complete trust that Life produces something like it (or better than I imagined it) and gives it back to me.

Chapter 15

STEP FIVE: LET IT BE SO

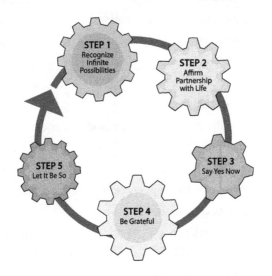

STEP 1
Recognize
Infinite
Possibilities

STEP 2
Affirm
Partnership
with Life

STEP 3
Say Yes Now

STEP 4
Be Grateful

STEP 5
Let It Be So

STEP FOUR: Let: Life inspires me and its law responds to me. I return my words to Life's limitless operation. I let new possibilities match my new mindset. **Create:** Certainty that Life works according to its nature. **Generate:** Confidence that the co-creative partnership is expressing more good (for me and for all).

"Just like you don't hoist your sails to move the boat,
but to put yourself within reach of the wind."
—Mike Dooley, *Manifesting Change: It Couldn't Be Easier*

Everything Returns to the Source

Step Five ends the treatment as you began it, with the recognition that One Life is the source of everything visible and invisible.

Having immersed yourself *in* Life and realized your connection *with* your desire, return your affirmations *to* Life and its creativity. Recognize that the power of creativity is not yours, although your unity with it permits you to direct it. By Step Five, you have put yourself into a state of allowing and put out the welcome mat for Life to manifest what you desire.

Let's review the five steps with an example, so that you can see how everything returns to the source. In this example, let's say you desire greater abundance. Therefore, the purpose of this treatment is to align you with the source of abundance, putting you squarely in its flow and in its path of manifestation.

Once you recognize that abundance is the nature of Life (Step One), and whatever is Life's nature is your nature (Step Two), you acknowledge your inherent partnership with Life and become receptive to abundance in a new way. Whereas you may have previously allowed yourself to misjudge the availability of abundance or your worthiness to receive it, at this point all that is necessary is to understand that abundance *is* your nature.

Accepting the abundance you desire and deserve instills a new attitude and way of thinking (Step Three). In essence, you are saying yes to abundance and letting your thoughts generate an atmosphere and vibration of abundance. You feel naturally grateful (Step Four), not only for your new state of thinking but also for the abundance you expect as a result of your new attitude.

Finally, just as holding on to money too tightly will not allow it back into circulation, you want to loosen your grip on your thoughts about your rightful abundance. Holding on too tightly, whether from resistance to good or from lack of trust, interferes with Life's flowing nature. You conclude your treatment by confidently trusting Life to respond to your new thoughts and happy anticipation of new results (Step Five).

In this whole process of treatment, you ultimately recognize that Life is the source of your abundance and of all the good you desire. It is Life that makes everything possible. As a great teacher once said, "Of myself, I can do nothing." At the conclusion of this treatment, your life feels different to you because *you* are changed by it. The creative process is at work, responding to the new—abundant—you.

What's Yours? What's Life's?

This last step lets us surrender to the source of infinite possibilities. It is a demonstration of our faith in the creative process and a declaration of our partnership with Life. We recognize that, with all we have done (in thought, words, and actions), Life will do its part.

Our human ego tends to take all the credit. After all, it *is* your choice and your effort to change your thoughts, right? Yes, choice and effort are yours. But be clear about what is yours to do and what is Life's to do.

Life is as necessary to your creativity as you are to Life's expression and expansion. It is your oneness with Life that makes it possible for you to co-create the life you desire. The first two steps of treatment establish this sense of unity and partnership with Life. As you end your treatment, acknowledge Life's part and your part. It is like leaving an important meeting with an agreement about who is responsible for the next steps in moving the new project toward success. You do your part, and Life does its part. Take responsibility for what is yours to do—staying in alignment with your true, new self. Treatment shifts your thinking into this alignment.

It is equally important to affirm your confidence that Life does its part—operating according to principles and laws to demonstrate its nature of responsiveness, abundance, intelligence, and every other good quality—to express more Life through all creation, including *you*.

You can't sail your boat without the ocean to carry you and the wind to fill your sails.

Your job is to plant, weed, cultivate, and fertilize new thoughts and new possibilities. Life provides the soil and the rich medium for new life to grow and flourish. Do your part and move on. Trust the greater power of Life to work for you.

We do not live in a vacuum. We do nothing by ourselves. We live in a world in which everything is interconnected. When you recognize that there is a greater power behind everything you think and experience, you'll realize you have access to more potential than you ever imagined.

You *can* choose to go it alone and live your life as a sole proprietorship. Many people achieve success this way. But the journey isn't nearly as easy and the results aren't as fulfilling as when you consciously partner with Life. When you work together with Life, you are reassured that a partner is on your side, always supporting you and offering your highest good. Share, trust, and rely on Life as it relies on you to be the means of its expression and expansion.

Step Five sends the vibration of your words back to the source of their inspiration, for Life's full and powerful creativity. Proceed in complete confidence that you are in harmony with Life's nature, knowing that Life follows its own laws precisely, consistently, and reliably.

> "I rise up in the dignity and integrity of myself as a spiritual being, and I know that the power that supports this universe supports me, and I allow it to do just that."
>
> —Raymond Charles Barker, *365 Days of Richer Living*

Get Out of the Way

If you have lived by the old Have-Do-Be model of living, you may have learned to control conditions (and control others) in order to get what you want. There is no need to have a tight hold on anything, because you can trust Life to create it with you and for you. Holding, controlling, and manipulating create resistance, which gets in the way of your dreams.

"The only person you can trust is yourself." "If you want something done right, you have to do it yourself." These are common statements about control. They may imply confidence, but they exclude Life and its infinite potential.

The Be-Do-Have model doesn't require control. It focuses on responsibility, commitment, intention, and partnership with Life. In this model, you can choose to direct your life, follow your true nature, and let your dream guide your intentions. You can include Life in your dreams, and Life will support you and deliver your good. Instead of thinking it is you doing all the work and making everything happen, let Life's creative soil grow your seed. Instead of thinking you know the only right way, the only solution, let Life's infinite intelligence reveal your next brilliant solution. Do your part, and then get out of the way and let Life help you.

Life Knows What It's Doing

Not only is Life the source of your ideas, but it can also take your new ideas and give them further expansion and expression. This is its nature. Trust Life to act according to its nature. It will not fail you. It will not exclude you from its activity, because you are forever inseparable from it.

Trust Life to help you and to hold for you a greater possibility than you can see for yourself. It does not actually need your trust to do this, because this is its nature. Your trust is for you. When you trust Life, you become receptive to its nature as your nature. When you trust Life, you harmonize with it, eliminating any sense of alienation or powerlessness. In your own mind, eliminate any sense of separation *from* Life and any resistance that may have been caused by your lack of trust *in* Life.

Letting Go

In this step, many people choose to say, "I let go" as a way to relinquish control. While in Step Three "I let go" referred to letting go of old patterns of thinking and being, in this step it means letting this entire treatment go back to its source. It represents letting it go to dance with creativity, instead of holding it tight and smothering it.

Your partnership with Life makes it unnecessary to struggle, force, or manipulate anything or anybody to do or to be what you want. Let Life orchestrate the potential in all that is visible and invisible, in every condition and every person, to manifest according to your desires. Trust Life to determine how to satisfy the good of all (with harm to none).

It is tempting to presume that Step Five means you're completely finished with your work. It's true that you're releasing your words back to Life's infinite creativity to activate new possibilities. However, resist the urge to rush through this step by just saying, "I let go." There's more to letting go. Even a gardener sometimes spends more time weeding than planting.

Michael Bernard Beckwith, founder of the Agape International Spiritual Center, teaches that 100 percent of our growth involves letting go of the belief that we must pump in from the outside the qualities we feel we lack to fulfill our life's purpose. The truth, he says, is that all we need to fulfill our unique purpose has already been implanted within us.

It's safe to say that all of us have accumulated limited beliefs and wrong ideas about what Life is and how Life works. We've narrowed our concept of who we are and our rightful place as Life's partner. We've fostered anger, frustration, judgment, guilt, blame, and shame for so long that we aren't aware that these have become our automatic responses to the world around us. We may work at jobs we don't like for reasons that don't make us feel empowered. We may spend our days feeling insignificant and hopeless while we are simultaneously surrounded by astounding beauty and creativity.

For every kind of predicament or challenge, there is an example of someone who leaped beyond limitations. These people show us that the boundaries in our lives start in our heads. If we would see rightly, we would notice that they teach us that we're all connected to Life's infinite possibilities.

At the center of your being, you have everything you need. If this isn't your experience, then letting go is not the smallest step, and it is possibly even the most important. Letting go of beliefs, words, emotions, or anything that creates a sense of limitation may be the tipping point toward your better life.

We often think there's something outside us that we need in order to be happy and healthy. It's a feeling like something's missing. On the contrary, nothing is missing. You are connected to the rich, limitless source of everything. If anything is missing, it's your awareness and appreciation of your connection with Life. The solution is to realize that happiness is an inside job and you've got exactly what you need within you already. Everything awaits your decision to let new possibilities serve your happiness.

For example, when we are lonely, it may feel like we are missing love, and so we go in search of it instead of discovering the bottomless wellspring of love inside us. In truth, love isn't missing at all, but rather waiting for your recognition of it to come forward. It's like parents who believe they give their first child all the love they have. Yet when the next baby arrives, suddenly more love surges forth from the wellspring that responds when we call on it.

Or, when we are broke, we feel like we lack money, and we search for the means to get more. In truth, we're poor inside because we do not see the sea of abundance in which we live. Abundance is Life's nature, and it's our nature, too. A drop of water in the ocean does not lack wetness or have to search for the experience of being wet, or for any other quality of the ocean itself.

When anything seems missing, we want to go find what will complete us. But what we seek is right where we are. We must let go of whatever stands between our complete immersion in life and our experience of it. Don't be distracted by trying to find what completes you. The real goal of letting go is to realize who and what you are. The result is loving yourself as Life loves you and allowing yourself all the good Life already offers you.

Turn It Over (to Life) and Turn It Up (to a Higher Frequency)

No matter who puts their kayak into the river, the river does not hesitate, withhold its power, or change its flow. It acts according to its nature for everyone alike.

When we submit something to Life, Life takes it into its flow and movement toward manifestation. However, we must submit. Just as we allow our kayak to follow the flow of the river, we submit our new ideas and our desires to the flow of Life and let Life take them directly toward manifestation. Life leads us to infinite potential.

> "There is no limit to the good which is mine. Everywhere I go I see this good, I feel it, I experience it. It presses itself against me, flows through me, expresses itself in me, and multiplies itself around me."
>
> —Ernest Holmes, author of *A New Design for Living*

Having done our part to align with Life's higher vibration, having dreamed bigger and created something we have claimed as ours, having given thanks for the creation that is happening in this present moment that is ripe with creativity, we let Life do its part. We allow the river to carry us and our dreams forward.

Life offers more good than you have ever experienced and more good than you have ever imagined.

Submitting to the flow of Life does nothing to Life, but it registers within us a sense of partnership and co-creation. "By myself I can do nothing" acknowledges the power by which miracles are made possible. Understanding this partnership with the source of everything makes anything that constitutes a better life possible for you, too.

Essentially, the last step represents a form of surrender. You are not surrendering to something in a way that feels defeated or subservient. On the contrary, you are surrendering *up to* a greater and limitless vision of yourself and Life. This kind of surrender isn't throwing in the towel but rather submitting to a promotion of your greater self. Your greater self operates at a higher frequency.

Surrendering is not letting go of anything.
It is letting it go *to* a new and better possibility.
It's not giving *in;* it's giving *in to* something new.

Just as you began this process by declaring your bigger concept of Life, in this last step, your bigger concept of Life is now a part of you. You have made a shift that cannot be undone or taken back. You have said yes to Life in a bigger way, and Life's creativity is off and running with it.

When you change, Life changes around the new version of you.

Upon completing the Five Step Treatment, go about your everyday life in your new state. Act in accordance with your higher vibration and in accordance with your desires that are presently unfolding. Surrender into Life's bigger possibilities and go about your new way while Life fulfills its share of the partnership—to respond to the new you in a new way. Live in great expectation of what is around every corner.

Something wonderful is happening in your Life right now, so go look for it. Look *from* a higher level of vibration, a level at which more is possible than ever before. In this new place, there *is* more good than you can see or imagine, and it is happening right now. It is making its way into your imagination, expanding you into a new intention.

Life Spirals Upward and Outward

Life's dynamic activity is often illustrated as a circle, a continuous movement back to a starting point to repeat its pattern. There are many examples of this concept in nature. The four seasons. The life cycle of plants. The movement of water from the atmosphere to Earth and back.

It may be more accurate to depict the activity of Life as a spiral, a circular motion that returns not quite to the same point of its beginning but to a slightly different and higher place that represents a *new* path. The spiral reflects Life's nature to expand itself without repeating itself.

Evolution represents the spiral of upward and outward progression toward new forms of Life. As we have seen, every era brings new discoveries and inventions at an increasing rate.

> "Life creates more possibilities as it engages with opportunities. There are no 'windows of opportunity,' narrow openings in the fabric of space-time that soon disappear forever. Possibilities beget more possibilities; they are infinite."
>
> —Margaret Wheatley, author of *So Far from Home: Lost and Found in Our Brave New World*

In the past, it may have been your pattern to keep repeating undesirable experiences, but that is not your nature. As you make new choices, set new intentions, and co-create new experiences, you can experience life in new and expansive ways. With each new thought, you develop a new mindset. After all, if Life's nature is a spiral, that is your nature, too.

The purpose of the Five Step Treatment is to create a shift in your thinking. In this way, you are not the exact same person after a Five Step Treatment, but rather a new and better version of yourself. You are happier, healthier, more at peace, more creative, or more of whatever you shifted into being during the process of treatment. More precisely, since this process has created a change within you, you are a changed person. You are in a new place of your own spiraling growth and evolution.

Whatever your initial goal of treatment, by Step Five, you arrive not only at a place of completion but at a new place of inquiry, desire, and inspiration. Whether or not you were able to fully heal your mindset of false obstacles and restore your inherent wholeness, you have become a new person, ready for something new.

Each new treatment is an opportunity to move yourself into a greater alignment with the source of infinite good, a greater expectation of possibilities, and a greater confidence in your co-creative partnership. Each treatment becomes an upward spiral into a higher vibrational energy and an expanded sense of yourself and of your significance in the world.

Faith and Certainty Breed Confidence

What happens when you know Life is on your side, in your corner, working for you and making everything available to you? You feel supported, that's what. No longer are you pushing a boulder uphill or swimming against the current. You're flowing in a river that's moving you with it, by its power, not yours.

It is said that faith is about what we hope for in the absence of evidence. Faith is our belief in that which we cannot see—the invisible side of Life. We have faith until we see evidence, and then we become certain. Certainty demands proof. Faith may be what we have before we step off a cliff; certainty is what we gain after we gather evidence of what comes next.

At this point, you're willing to work with the principles and techniques in this book on faith. Something within you agrees with truth as it's been presented. Your great desire for something better fuels your faith that something better is indeed possible.

You've been encouraged to create your own experiment in order to test these principles and techniques. The point is to move from faith to certainty. When you begin to experience more good in your life, your faith will grow. When you see the things you desire show up, the actual demonstration will build certainty. In your own life experiment, your results will build greater certainty about Life and your relationship to it. Your experience will be your proof.

Step Five lets you flow with Life, in its current of unconditional love and unending process of giving. Step Five lets you stop pushing the boulder or swimming the wrong way. In fact, Step Five lets you walk away from your treatment and go on with your day. Let go of the idea that you have to hold on to your words or try hard to do something after your treatment. There's absolutely no reason to scrunch up your face or grunt with effort. Relax. Let your words create, let your new mindset be Life's new assignment and let Life work for you.

Feel confident. Move on. You've got new possibilities to entertain.

Yeah, But . . .

Q: What do I do now? How long do I wait? What do I look for?
A: The Five Step Treatment brings you to certainty at best, and hope at the least. With that in mind, go about your business. See your world from a fresh viewpoint. Count on the new (truer) you to carry you into a new experience of life.

However, if your mind is racing, worrying, wondering, you are thwarting your good Five Step Treatment. The Buddhist term "monkey mind" describes thoughts that are unsettled, jumping nonstop and out of control, like an undisciplined monkey in the forest. When this happens, do another treatment or anything that lets you feel assured that something new is coming. Spend time in nature, meditate, or visualize what you desire, and act as if your good is already yours (because it is). All of these activities take your mind away from limiting thoughts and return it to expansive thoughts aligned with Life. They generate a vibration toward your intention.

Whether you see anything different or not, something *is* different—*you* are different. It is a scientific fact that the energy of your vibration affects all that is around you. Do not be discouraged by appearances. Appearances change constantly, even if so slightly as to be indistinguishable. Life's nature does not change. Keep your thoughts on the side of Life and not appearances—this is your new rock, your new solid foundation.

Meanwhile, go on an expedition to find more good and more to be grateful for. Maintain the high vibration.

Q: With all that is happening in the world around me, I'm supposed to trust Life? It's risky to trust. It makes me vulnerable. It sets me up to fail. The bottom line is, trusting always backfires.

A: Bingo! Nothing reveals your beliefs quite as clearly as a highly charged reaction when you are presented with the opposite of it. It is as if someone has pushed a button in you that makes you recoil and snap right back.

Observe the limiting beliefs within this question: "Trusting Life is risky." "I'm vulnerable to failure." Consider whether you have these beliefs and whether they have created negative experiences that continue to reinforce the belief.

How far do you trust Life? Apply the following questions to help discern a limiting belief from an expansive one, discern falsehood from truth, or discern what is Life's nature or your nature from what is not:

Does believing this create more Life, or does it limit Life?

Does this make me feel more alive or less alive?

Does this make me feel bigger or smaller?

Would believing this make me feel more free?

Life does not fail any part of its creation. The bare trees in the winter are never separate from the Life that was present in their blossoms the previous spring. Life doesn't leave the caterpillar without the potential for complete transformation. Life never backfires, and Life never lets us down.

Are you willing to consider that your perception of Life is what has failed you and made you feel vulnerable to further disappointment? Take a close look at the source of your fear, and see it with new eyes. See the presence of Life, not the absence.

The challenges of the world have been created by beliefs in the absence of Life, not in its abundant and powerful presence. Look at the world from the perspective of infinite abundance, and you'll see a new world with new, abundant possibilities.

Q: My desires aren't showing up. Where's my "better life"?

A: The creative process works; it's working right now. Not seeing it does not mean it's not happening. Your resistance and frustration create more to resist and be frustrated about.

When all the trees are bare in the winter, do you think Life left them? Do you throw a tantrum because the leaves fall off the trees or the flowers are not blossoming according to your schedule? If you can trust Life to manage the perfect pattern of seasons, can you believe the same is happening for you? Keep cultivating your mindset. Be patient. As they say, Rome wasn't built in a day.

Take a look at what *is* showing up. It might not be as you expected, but if you look at it rightly, you can find how something better is included in it. Whatever shows up will also lead to something else.

At some point, you might find yourself experiencing something you never dreamed, or something you forgot you once wanted.

Here's a story about my client Mo. I helped him create a life he loved, addressing every aspect: health, wealth, love, and happiness. He focused on the qualities that gave him fulfillment and expanded his beliefs and his expectations. One by one, each part of his life began to reflect his expansion and the qualities he desired.

Mo finally achieved the wealth to purchase his dream home. When he found it, he recalled a time when he dreamed of a better lifestyle but didn't know how to create it. He told me that he used to visualize a home just like the one he was now buying. For Mo, new pieces of his better life made him so happy that he nearly forgot about his dream . . . until it showed up.

SAMPLE WORDING FOR STEP FIVE

I release my words, knowing my thoughts, as my words, are powerful and met by a power that is greater than any condition.

I put my faith in truth and law and know they create my conditions. I do my part and have confidence that Life responds to me according to its abundant, responsive, and expansive nature.

What I believe is creative, and the words I speak activate a power that is already creating new form and experience.

I trust the creative law to deliver my experiences into the form I seek, or better. I trust Life to present

(continued on next page)

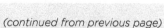

(continued from previous page)

me with the highest good, according to my dreams and desires.

Having affirmed what I know to be true, I let go to Life and its immutable law to respond in kind. What I give to Life, Life gives to me. These words do not return to me unanswered.

I entrust these words back to the source that invited and inspired them. I do my part and expect Life to prove to me its part, mirroring back to me in form and experience what I now believe and accept.

I surrender my words up to Life's greater intelligence and loving-kindness. Life is my happy and willing partner, producing for me according to my desires. I look for this—or something better that matches the qualities I seek—as it becomes real in my experience.

Chapter 16

MORE ABOUT TREATMENT

Getting Started

Here are two forms to help get you started doing your own power-ful Five Step Treatments. The first form is the Preparation for Treat-ment. Use it to get more clear about the purpose of your treatment and the changes you want to create. It is important to uncover the beliefs that are contributing to what you want to change, and to iden-tify a better belief that will help create what you do want. This form will encourage you to find the qualities and feelings associated with your desires. All of these elements will help you create an effective Five Step Treatment.

The second form is a Simplified Five Step Treatment. This form guides you to create your own Five Step Treatment, using the infor-mation from Preparation for Treatment.

Following the forms is a sample preparation and a sample treatment to show you how to use the forms to begin creating your own treatments. In the last part of this book, there are other treatments for changing your thoughts (and activating an outer change) regarding conditions and experiences. As you become more familiar with treatments and experienced in using them, you will be able to speak your own treatments with spontaneity, feeling, and conviction.

Preparation for Treatment

✾ **The purpose of my treatment:**

_____

_____

_____

✾ **I choose to change my experience:**
From this:

_____

To this:

_____

✾ **Here are beliefs that might be creating the condition** (as it has been) that I now wish to change. I am willing to release them now:

_____

_____

_____

_____

_____

_____

_____

_____

_____

✿ **Here are beliefs that support the new condition I desire.**
These new beliefs align with the qualities and nature of Life (hint:
new, empowering beliefs to create what you do want are often the
opposite of the limiting beliefs that created what you don't want):

_____

_____

_____

_____

_____

_____

_____

_____

_____

✤ **These are the qualities of Life I want to experience** (examples: joy, balance, abundance, love, peace, health, wholeness, creativity, wisdom, support, freedom, comfort, understanding, acceptance, kindness, generosity, trust, authenticity, beauty, ease, grace, inspiration, order, success):

_____

_____

_____

_____

_____

_____

✤ **This is how these new conditions will make me feel** (examples: happy, calm, prosperous, loved, peaceful, vibrant, strong, confident, alive, eager, optimistic, empowered, connected, grateful, playful, centered, renewed, enthusiastic, blissful, whole):

_____

_____

_____

_____

✤ I am willing to feel this now and see this quality of Life in my own Life now. I am willing to allow this new experience of Life—or something better. I let it be so.

A Simplified Five Step Treatment

✸ **Life is** (name the quality or nature of Life desired. Examples: balanced, flowing, joyful, whole, abundant, loving, creative, light, orderly, harmonious. Affirm universal truths about Life.):

_____

_____

_____

_____

_____

_____

✸ **I am** (name the qualities and feelings that unify you with Life. State your partnership with Life and how you feel you are connected, in terms of what you desire and choose to believe. Affirm new beliefs about yourself.):

_____

_____

_____

_____

✸ **I say yes to** (claim the good as though it already exists, because it does. Describe your good in expansive ways. Affirm new beliefs about your good.):

_____

_____

_____

_____

✸ **I am grateful for** (name the good you claimed, and appreciate the new and better mindset that allows you to accept your good, because it's already yours. Add your enthusiasm and expectation.):

_____

_____

_____

_____

_____

✸ **I release these words back to the powerful activity of Life.** I trust creativity is happening. I let Life do its part. What I desire is already so. I intend to find evidence of it. I let it be so, and so it is! (Use these or your own words.):

_____

_____

_____

_____

_____

Preparation for Treatment (Sample)

Note: Notice below how the word "want" was replaced with a more empowering word, to eliminate the idea of wanting and avoid creating more wanting.

The purpose of my treatment: a better job
I choose to change my experience.
From this: I don't like my job I don't feel appreciated, it doesn't interest me, and it doesn't pay well.
To this: I require a job I love so much, it makes me excited to go each day.

Here are beliefs that might be creating the experience:
I don't deserve the best. I don't have much to offer. Other people have money, not me.

Here are beliefs that support the new experience I desire:
All that is Life nature is my nature, and that includes expression and abundance. I deserve what I desire. I have something special to offer in a way no one else can.

These are the qualities of Life I want to experience:
Joy, abundance, creativity, purpose, appreciation, acknowledgment, success, connection.

This is how these new conditions will make me feel:
Happy, content, jubilant, grateful, supported.

I am willing to feel this now and see this quality of Life in my own life now. I am willing to allow this new experience of Life—or something better.

A Simplified Five Step Treatment (Sample)

Note: Feel free to add your own wording in the samples provided under the topic of each step. Copy the words that feel right to you, change them, or write your own.

Life is: Life is creative. Life creates and gives unconditionally to what it creates. Life is abundant. Life makes more than plenty available—infinite good and infinite possibilities.

I am: I am Life's expression and Life's inlet and outlet of creativity. Life's nature is my true nature. My nature is abundance and creativity. There is purpose for me and my gifts. There are possibilities that suit my desires to express my uniqueness in the world. My unity with Life connects me with good of all kinds.

I say yes to: I accept Life's good as a job that suits me. I let go of the beliefs that limit me and keep me from being happy. I deserve what I desire. I have something special to offer. I allow Life to guide me toward my perfect work, opening doors and creating new opportunities. My perfect work is exhilarating, creative, and rewarding. It uses my best gifts and lets me shine like the sun. Possibilities are endless, and so I accept the possibility that's perfect for me.

I am grateful for: I am grateful for my right and perfect work. My heart is made happy by my new outlook and expectation. With Life on my side, I am glad for a power that's helping me create more than I could on my own. I am grateful for opportunities to share my unique gifts and talents.

I release these words back to the powerful activity of Life: I trust Life to create the conditions in my life, including a new job, to match my new thoughts and beliefs. I have activated something new and expect results. I let Life present me with my highest good in the form of work. What I desire exists, is meant for me, and is making its way to me now.

Every Treatment a Success

Since the purpose of treatment is to realize that what you desire is already available to you, satisfaction is built into the Five Step Treatment.

Treatment breaks down resistant thoughts that are blocking your desires and realigns your thoughts to let the creative process attract your desires. In essence, treatment is a way to replace Life-depleting thoughts (contributing to what you *don't want*) with Life-affirming thoughts (supporting what you *do want*).

Step by step, treatment encourages you toward a bigger picture of the life you desire. The big picture contains the qualities of Life that are important to you and the ways in which Life can help fulfill you. You get to determine what constitutes your better life (or something better from Life's storehouse of possibilities).

Each treatment may vary in its purpose, according to your daily needs and your intention for guidance and clarity. But if you hold the big picture of what you desire in mind at all times, your treatments can lead you toward your dreams. If each step forward represents success, so does each treatment constitute success by its own design.

Treatments Are Unique and Cumulative

In the movie *Groundhog Day*, Bill Murray plays a television weatherman who travels with his crew to Punxsutawney, Pennsylvania, to cover the annual recognition of this holiday. Each morning he awakens only to realize it's Groundhog Day—again. This happens the next day and the next day and so on. However, he experiences the same Groundhog Day differently each day, because *he's different*. With every replay of the same day, he experiences it in a new way, discovers something new, and becomes a new person. Each day brings him closer to experiencing his true nature in a way he never thought possible. Eventually, he finds the love he always wanted.

The movie illustrates how we can experience everything with a new awareness when we realize that each experience changes us. Coincidentally, this movie illustrates the principles of the Five Step Treatment, as the main character ultimately learns that the good he seeks is available to him when he allows himself to be receptive to it.

It is impossible to do the same treatment twice, because each time you have even the slightest shift in your thoughts, your next treatment will come from the new you. Therefore, each treatment is unique and none is alike. In other words, you cannot fail. Each treatment builds upon the ones that came before it.

According to neuroscientists, consistent thought creates grooves in our brain, like well-traveled paths. As we think something over and over, the process of the thought creates patterns for neuron charges to follow. In essence, by consistent repetition we create habits of thought in the same way in which we create habits in our behavior.

Repetition creates a groove of new thinking while it lessens our resistance to new ideas and bold dreams. As we repeatedly visualize our dream, our neurons form a familiar path to them. With no resistance and greater certainty, our thoughts move into autopilot, requiring less and less effort to follow a path to our desires.

Five Step Treatments can vary each day. One day, your treatment may focus on achieving peace of mind. Another day, your purpose may be to become more willing to receive the complete dream you have in mind. All treatments are good if they move you into a new mindset and acceptance of Life's good as your good. If all of your treatments contribute to your new mindset, you are on the right track. You're partnering with Life to co-create your desire.

When Treatment Doesn't (Appear to) Work

It is common to conclude that treatment doesn't work if it doesn't manifest what you want, the way you want, when you want it. But the question is not whether treatment is working. Treatment works. Many, many people have proven it to themselves, and you can, too. So, what *is* actually happening if you're not experiencing what you're treating for, and how can you adjust your thinking so you can experience it?

Laws are infallible. If a bridge collapses, it is not that the laws of physics failed to hold it up. If your answer to a math problem is incorrect, the laws of mathematics did not fail. If you are not creating what you want, it is not because Life and its principles and processes aren't working for you. However, several things may be contributing to your disappointment.

Let's look at one possible scenario. Suppose you have treated for living in your perfect new home. One day, you discover that the house of your dreams is actually for sale. You make an offer and wait expectantly to hear that the house is yours. If your offer is not accepted, did Life ignore your Five Step Treatment for the home you desired, deserved, and expected? The simple answer is that Life's responsive nature is infallible.

Maybe you limited your receptivity to only one possibility. Much like a horse that wears blinders, your sight was closed to other options. While you expected something very specific, Life always has your best interests at heart and may be leading you to a different—and better—home to satisfy you.

Reevaluate what *is* showing up in your life. If Life is giving you something other than what you were expecting, find the potential gifts in it. What you receive might simply represent a step toward your desire, rather than the full-blown desire itself.

Don't be impatient with the creative process. There is an orderly and sequential process of your own growth toward your better life. If you desire something for which you are not ready, you are trying to manifest something that is out of sequence in your perfect upward spiral of growth.

What you get mirrors your inner thoughts and beliefs. In the process of changing yourself, you may not immediately get what you desire. Keep working on replacing limited beliefs with empowering ones. The impetus that compels you to desire something is the same impetus that is evolving the experience for you. Your desire for it indicates your readiness "toward" it, and Life will respond with something closer to it—when you believe in it.

Another reason you don't get exactly what you want is when it is better for someone else. Remember that all laws work perfectly and fairly. Life's giving nature includes everyone. There is an infinite inventory from which Life produces good for all.

Let's apply some of these possibilities to the example of buying the house of your dreams. Maybe the other prospective buyers who made an offer on the same house expected the house to fulfill *their* dream. If their offer was accepted, that would mean that the house *was* theirs, in principle, to have as part of their expression and expansion—and therefore, despite your perceptions, it was *not* yours to have. This doesn't mean you didn't deserve it. Maybe the house of your dreams wasn't this one but another one that you haven't found yet but that suits you *better.*

To usurp someone else's good indicates a belief in scarcity, as if there is not enough to go around. If you become resentful that your offer wasn't accepted, your resentment can create a new obstacle to receiving what you do want. If this sounds like you, consider doing a treatment to change *these* beliefs into beliefs that include plenty of good for everyone.

Life gives fairly and unconditionally to everyone. Life gives lovingly and freely, but you will only attract that which matches the vibration of your mindset (i.e., like attracts like). Want for others what you want for yourself, and by so doing, you will replicate the loving and giving nature of Life for all. Life seeks to express more of itself. Trust Life to support you in ways that will satisfy you, even when that satisfaction comes in unexpected ways and by a circuitous path.

Life supports the highest and greatest good for everyone alike. Giving consideration to others is another way to side with Life and all it encompasses. Do not leave others out of your better life and your desires. Want the good for others that you want for yourself.

What Treatment Is Not

Treatment is not a way to appease, negotiate, bargain, or plead with; nor is it an outlet to beg, blame, or change Life.

Treatment is not a way to manipulate or change others.

Treatment is not a replacement for other forms of healing or other ways in which Life supports you. For example, in achieving health, treatment does not replace doctors. Doctors and nurses are only a few of the possibilities in which Life supports you. In achieving prosperity, treatment does not replace responsible financial management. When you pay bills, be aware of the ways in which Life supports you and the companies and services that provide what you require. In short, don't count on treatment alone. Keep your eyes open to how Life flows good to you.

Treatment is not positive thinking, wishful thinking. After all, you don't flip the light switch and hope the light turns on (if it's properly connected). Your expectation is based on the proper application of the law of electricity. In the same way, treatment is a proper use of Life's invisible law of responsiveness. Life's immutable operation makes wishing unnecessary.

Treatment is not denial thinking, head-in-the-sand avoidance, or willing things away. Instead, acknowledge the presence of Life in any situation and "treat" yourself to become aware of Life's power within you to choose the thoughts that support new, and better, conditions.

Treatment is not denying the reality of any experience. Each experience you have is a real one; there is no need to deny it. However, you can deny the power you give to any belief that manifests suffering of any kind. Suffering is not Life's nature, and it isn't your nature either. If you were experiencing physical pain from an injury, you wouldn't deny your pain, but you could deny that you believe pain is necessary. In fact, you might follow your denial with a bold affirmation that Life's energy is present in all your cells, revitalizing you from the inside out.

Treatment is not words spoken without feeling or without faith. Speak with the greatest conviction you can muster, using only words you *can* believe.

Treatment is not effective if you don't believe in it. You cannot receive anything you don't believe. Believe that what you desire is possible and available, and know that treatment is a means toward achieving it.

What Treatment Is

Treatment is recognizing awe-inspiring truths and the perfect patterns that already exist in your life as an expression of Life.

Treatment is aligning yourself in oneness with all that gives and all that creates and realizing you are essential to Life's expression.

Treatment is a method for clearing your mind of false and disempowering beliefs.

Treatment is consciously taking your attention away from any (visible) condition that you don't want and putting your attention on the (invisible) qualities of Life that you do want, in order to allow them to manifest into new, and better, conditions.

Treatment is letting Life guide you in directing the creative process to produce what will make you happy, without fixed outcomes, so you can allow for something better.

Treatment is a technique for directing the creative process, setting creation into motion through an orderly sequence of progress based on universal principles and truths.

Treatment is a way to open your mind, expand your awareness, accept truth, become more willing, allow new possibilities, and become more receptive, so Life can express more fully through you.

Treatment is a powerful tool to reinforce forgiveness, gratitude, eliminate judgment, and build compassion in order to replicate Life's loving nature in your own life.

Summary of Part III

Treatment is a technique that helps you build awareness that everything that is Life's nature is your true, limitless, and creative nature.

Treatment creates a shift in your mindset that lets you welcome all your desire into your experience now, activating the creative process to produce it for you. Treatment is a way to become receptive to the ideas and possibilities that lead to your happiness.

Treatment facilitates growing your idea *of* yourself, expanding your receptivity to greater possibilities *for* yourself.

Treatment helps you shift your attention and thoughts away from what you don't want and what is limiting you (negative, resistant energy) to what you do want and what will help you (positive, allowing energy). It raises your vibration into the level of new possibilities and generates a creative, expansive energy of expectation.

Treatment provides satisfaction within the treatment itself, allowing you to realize that what you desire is already available to you. Your new mindset activates the creation of new forms and experiences.

What's Next?

Part III was all about the Five Step Treatment: what it is and how to use it. This daily tool shapes your thoughts and your energy so that Life's creative process can reveal the forms and experiences that match your desires.

Part IV provides a collection of actual Five Step Treatments. As you practice creating your own unique treatments, use these to address daily issues or personal intentions. They are meant to inspire and lift you into your own thoughts, your own words, and your own possibilities.

Part IV

TREAT YOURSELF TO SOMETHING BETTER

[change • possibilities]

Chapter 17

TREATMENTS FOR YOUR BETTER LIFE

THE TREATMENTS ON THE FOLLOWING pages are meant to help you on your way to whatever a better life means to you. If you know what you need next, treat for it. If you don't know, treat to receive guidance from the infinite wisdom that is already within you.

Life waits on you, offering to you everything you desire and everything you require. These treatments can help you heal what is in the way and activate something good to come your way. Use these treatments to shift your thoughts, your perspective, and your willingness. Allow your true self to shine and allow Life to express more good—through you, for you, and because of you.

Treat Yourself to Embrace Change

Purpose of this treatment: To stop letting my fear of change get in the way of what I want. To realize change is required for something better to emerge. To embrace change as a stepping-stone toward my dreams. To become more willing.

Step one: There is One Life. Creativity is its nature. Change is its nature. Every day is an entirely new day. Every day represents change. Every new thing is evidence of how change is natural. Growth and expansion require change.

Step two: I am part of Life's dynamic movement. I am part of the change that happens all around me. The cells of my body change daily. My thoughts change. As my true self emerges, some part of me changes and I become more than I thought before.

Step three: I let go of my fear of change and fear of the unknown. I let go of my resistance to change and feel it being replaced by the energy of allowing. As I realize Life is always for me, there is nothing to fear.

I side with Life and I embrace change. I let change be my tool for growth and more good. I am guided rightly, in ways that are unmistakably beckoning me forward. My highest good is clear. I welcome changes that bring me closer to my dreams.

Today I see the dynamic movement of Life. I find new ways and new views. I entertain new thoughts. My allowing state makes me feel excited for the good that is coming to me.

Step four: I am thankful for Life's spiraling, growing nature. I am grateful for my willingness to change. I am grateful for how change inspires me and guides me to a greater expression of my true self and a greater experience of my good.

Step five: I let Life bring more change to me. My receptivity to something new brings it to me.

Treat Yourself to More Good

Purpose of this treatment: To realize I am the co-creator of my good. To experience more good of all kinds. To increase my expectations and my experience of good.

Step one: Life is everywhere present, all-powerful, and all-knowing. Its presence creates unceasing expression and expansion, whether seen or unseen, known or unknown. Life is infinitely creative.

Step two: This Life includes me. Just as a drop in the ocean is never separate from the ocean, I am never separate from Life. I do not have to include myself in Life and its infinite abundance, because, like the drop, I am already immersed in it. I do not have to create my good, because it already surrounds me and issues forth from within me. There is more good than I can see and more good than I can imagine, and it is being created right where I am now.

Step three: I release any belief that my good depends on any condition or circumstance. Nothing must change in my outer world for me to experience more good, because my thoughts create my experience.

I accept more good. I feel its flow and the joy of participating in its circulation. I accept abundant good in all ways. No matter what I thought yesterday, I think more today.

I feel the flow of good throughout every part of my life. Ideas pour forth from me. Love emanates from me and overflows onto everyone I meet. Love greets me and holds the door for me. Ease and grace carry me through each day. Miracles sprinkle themselves at my feet. A carpet of good appears beneath my every step. The fragrance of joy follows in my wake.

Step four: I am grateful for my expanded thinking and receptivity to more good. I am grateful for all the good that is and all the good that is becoming. Life is good.

Step five: I am Life's partner in co-creating more good in the world. As I look for good, I know Life's nature is to show me what I believe and expect. I hold Life accountable for demonstrating its nature—and my true nature—to me.

Treat Yourself to New Possibilities

Purpose of this treatment: To expand my thoughts and beliefs. To let go of limitations. To accept new possibilities of all kinds.

Step one: There is only One Life. It is limitless. No one can conceive of all that Life encompasses. Since nothing exists outside of Life, every possibility already exists right now.

Step two: Since I exist within Life, unified with Life, its possibilities are my possibilities. There is more available for me in the invisible field than in the visible world around me. As I open myself to receive more, there is nothing that stops more good from being revealed to me.

Step three: I release any thoughts of being small, of being less than my true self. Life doesn't limit me, and I won't limit myself anymore. No matter what I have ever been told, I am more than I have believed.

I am willing to grow my thoughts into a bigger idea of myself. From this moment on, I claim I deserve whatever I choose. I allow my gifts to grow and reveal their magnificence. I let my light shine brighter than ever. There are possibilities in the invisible that match my new, brilliant vibration. Right now, they are coming to me because I am attracting them. I am a galvanizing energy of something wonderful and new being born into creativity. There are amazing new ideas and experiences that require *me*.

As my partner in co-creating, Life has something in store for me that promises more good. The world is ready for what I have to give and to share. Now that I am open to new possibilities, all will benefit from my new state of being. This is my fulfillment.

It's a new world and a new day—because of who I am and because I am making a powerful decision to welcome something new.

Step four: I am grateful for my own willingness and my shift into openness. For whatever is coming to me, by means of me, I am already thankful. I feel giddy with anticipation of this good that is happening.

Step five: I release my word to Life's limitless creative activity. Around every corner, I expect something amazing. My open arms receive what Life is sending my way. A welcome mat for possibilities is at the door of my awareness.

Treat Yourself to Appreciating Yourself

Purpose of this treatment: To reverse my feelings of worthlessness. To find a reason that I matter and have purpose. To feel good about who I am. To start loving myself.

Step one: Life is all there is. This One Life creates and expresses its perfect qualities into the world. Life's nature is infinite creativity. Life expresses infinite variety and infinite possibilities. Since beauty is Life's nature, then beauty is in all things. Since Life is perfect, then everything created contains perfection. Life's loving nature permeates everything and everyone.

Step two: Since nothing is outside of Life, then I cannot be outside of Life. As Life is only good and creative and intelligent, then I cannot be separate from these qualities. What makes me unique makes me special. I am here, and so I must have purpose for being here.

Exactly as I am, Life seeks expression through me. Love breathes me and supports me. I am evidence of Life's unconditional love. Through me, love seeks to be expressed and experienced.

Step three: I let go of not feeling special. I let go of all the reasons I have created in my own mind to avoid being the special person I have always known deep down in my heart I am. I let go of my thoughts, beliefs, and experience of my past that have dragged me into a downward spiral. This ends now because I choose new thoughts today.

I let Life be my partner. I accept that I am here for the simple purpose of being me. I choose to love myself. I claim that there is something that makes me unlike any other, and this something proves my purpose. My existence proves that I am special. I let my light shine.

Already I feel something good and loving filling me within. Already I am hopeful for a new future because of the new—true—me. I like feeling special and worthwhile. My gifts and talents are being revealed, and I enjoy discovering them.

Step four: I feel so grateful for understanding there is a reason for me. I am thankful for this day, when I changed my thoughts and started allowing my true nature. I gladly anticipate the good that is being activated by my new awareness. I appreciate who I am, what I offer and the good that is being activated by my new thoughts.

Step five: My thoughts are creative, and my words have power. As I continue to make them stronger, I let Life prove them to me in form and experience. I go about my day as a new self—my true self—and I look forward to all the ways the world adjusts to me.

Treat Yourself to Letting Go

Purpose of this treatment: To release my bad feelings about another person. I want to feel reconciled and at peace within myself about what has transpired between us so that I may move on with my life, free of this obstacle and free to create something new.

Step one: There is only One Life. Its nature is to express itself into form. Every person is a unique and special expression of Life. We all share Life's qualities, even the air that gives us breath to live. Nothing separates any part or any person.

Step two: I am one with Life and everything created by Life. I cannot be separate from anyone else. We are all connected. We share so much. When I breathe, the air that gives me life also carries the joy, the pain, the love, and the anguish of others. My vibration touches another's, and theirs touches mine. We all want the same—to love and be loved. We all want to be accepted for who we are, exactly as we are, for our good qualities and for the ways we mistakenly hide our specialness.

Step three: No matter what I have ever done or will ever do, Life will never turn its back on me. Life embraces everyone. Even though I cannot change the past or what this person has done, I can choose a new future starting now.

Life accepts me and is always for me. Therefore, I choose to side with Life. I choose to wipe the slate clean and make this a new day that is untouched by the past. I choose to be compassionate. I choose to believe that no one would hurt another if they were not already hurting inside. I choose to end this cycle of hurt and take a stand for compassion.

I forgive myself for my mistakes, and I forgive others. I bless them and wish them good. In my blessing, I free them into a new vibration that allows Life to inspire them anew. I give of myself by giving to another.

Step four: I am grateful for this new way of being. It makes me feel lighter to dissolve old energy with love. I love my true self more because I share compassion with another.

Step five: My choices have already changed something in me. Whether my own eyes see evidence or not, I know my new choices allow this other person new and higher possibilities. As I let this go, I am certain that Life finds new ways to express through me a lighter and more loving me than I have ever been.

Treat Yourself to Wisdom

Purpose of this treatment: To receive answers to my questions, solutions to my problems, and clarity about whatever confuses me, distracts me, or clouds my thinking. I desire a clear message, as if receiving a note from Life.

Step one: Life is infinitely intelligent. There is nothing outside of Life's all-knowing nature. Confusion does not exist in Life's orderly operation. It orchestrates the planets and the stars of countless galaxies. It whispers to each and every flower all they require for a bravo performance.

Step two: Life informs every cell and organ and system in my body of exact assignments to make me alive. Every eventuality in my life already exists in Life's infinite possibilities. Therefore, the answers and solutions I seek are already available. My partnership with Life is my access pass to wisdom.

Step three: I am guided rightly by Life to receive everything I require to express myself as I desire. Life wants for me whatever I want for myself. Life supports me in all that I do. Therefore, I require guidance and clarity and I expect Life, as my partner, to provide it. As if with a single puff of breath, the clouds in my thoughts are dissolved and in their place appears a fresh, clear sky with a skywriting message just for me.

I am receptive to exactly what I need to know, and I accept Life's input. Thoughts come to me, opportunities present themselves, and things happen in ways that I perfectly understand as guidance meant for me. Life puts me right on track in whatever I need to know when I need to know it. I have the intelligence and knowledge and wisdom I require when I demand it.

Step four: I am thankful that my partnership with Life means I am never alone, and I am always supplied with whatever I require. As I keep focused on the qualities I want to express, I am grateful Life gives me the "hows" of achieving my better life and my dreams by guiding me forward.

Step five: With an open heart, an expectant mind, and eyes ready to see, I move forward with confidence that Life supports me and gives me whatever I require. I let Life make clear what is necessary for me to see and understand. We are partners, Life and I.

Treat Yourself to Creativity

Purpose of this treatment: To be filled with inspiration and ideas. To experience creativity as flowing, effortless, and fun ideas. To open to greater possibilities in my creative work beyond what I expect right now.

Step one: Everywhere is teeming evidence of Life's infinite creativity. Nature shows creativity in abundance, a changing display of beauty that becomes something entirely new, unduplicated, and breathtaking by the day and by the season. Life never lacks creativity. The sky is the most brilliant blue. The clouds are living works of art.

Step two: I am evidence of Life's infinite creativity. No matter how many millions have been before me, here I am, and no one is exactly like me. I am Life's work of art. Whatever I put my mind to is Life's creativity in action.

Step three: The same intelligence that inspired Michelangelo and Shakespeare is available to me. I am in partnership with the source of all ideas, brilliance, and creativity. It is as easy to receive a new thought about an invention or a solution as the idea about what to have for lunch today.

I let go of any preconceived or "average" thoughts that creativity is difficult to achieve or possible only by some. I let it be easy, and I choose to be a brilliant creator who is flooded with perfect ideas whenever I require them. Everywhere I look, I see creativity because I am a creator. In all that I do, my imagination is fed by a wellspring of possibilities.

Step four: I am grateful for this shift in mindset that lets me embrace being a creator and artist. My life is a celebration of possibility and potential. I am a magnet for creative opportunity that meets with success.

Step five: Yes, I am an artist of infinite potential. From this point on, I approach everything as an artist and allow Life to do the rest. As I turn on the faucet of creativity in my mind, I expect Life to flow amazing new ideas through me.

Treat Yourself to Perfect Work

Purpose of this treatment: Realize my desire for an ideal job that lets me express myself creatively and share and expand my gifts and talents. I want to feel appreciated and supported.

Step one: Life's nature is expressive and creative. Life creates and supports its creation. Life supports everything that expresses more Life.

There is no limit to Life's creativity. Life knows only to create more, to create anew, and to flow possibilities through every available channel of manifestation.

Step two: Life expresses by means of me. Life supports me. My connection with Life means there are places and opportunities for more Life to be expressed that match the gifts and talents I offer.

Step three: Life wants for me what I want for myself. I see myself in a job that is perfectly suited to me. I deserve work that interests and satisfies me.

I am receptive to my new work being revealed to me. I allow myself to be guided on a path to it. I am seeking it, and it is ready for me.

Obstacles melt away around me. Doors open to me. Clarity and intuition guide me. I attract the right opportunities, the right ideas, and the right resources that I require for my next and highest creative expression. Even now, I feel the excitement of doing work that uses all my gifts. Right now, the perfect job for me is seeking me as I am seeking it.

Step four: I am thankful for realizing everything is possible for me to have work that makes me happy and valued. I give thanks, know-

ing that the universe is rearranging itself right this minute to bring
my new job and me together.

Step five: I trust Life and its laws to deliver the work that is right for
me. I receive it with humbleness, with gratitude, and with love. I look
forward to all the ways my new job will allow me to give and to share
my true and best self. I release it into law and let Life do Life's work!

Treat Yourself to Better Health

Purpose of this treatment: To choose health. To experience
health. To replace beliefs about illness and disease with beliefs about
wholeness and well-being.

Step one: There is only One Life. It is good. It is intelligent and
dynamic. Life manages the infinite solar systems and also each single blade of grass. There is nothing outside of Life. All is contained
within its infinite field of power and possibilities.

Step two: I am one with Life. I live and breathe within an infinite field of possibilities. Possibilities are around me and within me.
There is a perfect intelligence within every cell, organ, and function
of my body. Life is alive in me.

Step three: I let go of old beliefs about illness and disease. They are
not inevitable. They are not my lot because of my gender, my culture,
my age, or any other definition. I let go of any limiting thoughts I
have about health and well-being.

In the field of possibility, perfect health, rejuvenation, remis-
sion, and healing already exist. Regardless of what my body shows

or what prevailing opinions predict for me, Life has more power and potential than anything that is visible now. The most powerful source of healing is Life within me.

My body is designed to heal and reveal vitality. My natural state is health. I accept healing and well-being in all ways and from all channels. Life is my source—it supports me and never fails me. I choose Life, and I choose health. I have more faith in Life than in any disease, because Life is my loving and creative partner. Life offers unlimited potential and possibilities. Life gives me more Life.

Step four: I am thankful for this breath I take as it reminds me I am alive. I am grateful for remembering Life's infinite power and possibilities. I am so grateful for my new mindset. How good it feels to affirm my partnership with Life in demonstrating my vitality.

Step five: My word has power and I release it now to the powerful activity of Life. My health and well-being are being restored by Life. I let my healing be so, by whatever forms or expertise Life uses for my benefit. The cells in my body jump for joy at my newfound perspective.

Treat Yourself to Wealth

Purpose of this treatment: To feel part of the flow and circulation of abundance. To allow wealth and prosperity as my true nature. To experience being fully supported financially so that all my needs are met. My better life includes financial well-being.

Step one: Life is abundant. Its nature is a constant profusion and flow of plenty. There is no such thing as a void in any part of

Life, because it is instantly and constantly filled with more Life, by Life. The oceans are kept filled. The skies are rich with every shade of blue.

Step two: My body is given every breath I need to feel alive. My heart never runs out of love; there is always more and more love that flows through me to fit every need for it and every place I choose to give it. Life's infinite energy provides everything required for me to experience my own rich aliveness.

Step three: It is not my nature to struggle. I exist in order to express and expand and create in the image of Life. Right now, I let go of any belief in poverty, lack, or limitation of any kind. I let go of my resistance to wealth and prosperity.

Life is the true source of all good, including money. Life is my partner, my banker, my lender, and part of every aspect of how money operates in my life. My beneficent partner approves me, supports me, and provides everything I require to experience my abundant nature.

I accept my rightful place in the flow of good. I accept money and financial well-being in my healthy, vibrant partnership with Life. Money flows to me effortlessly, as though I'm in the path of a flowing river. It is my friend; I welcome it and treat it like a precious guest, because it represents Life.

Plenty of money flows into my life to support every need and financial obligation. Plenty of money fills my portfolio, because it represents the riches and blessings that are mine every day I am alive with Life's magnificence. As my wealth grows, so grow all the ways I can give and share from my mindset of plenty.

Step four: I am grateful for my realization that it is my nature to live abundantly in this abundant world. I am grateful for all the ways I may use my wealth to distribute more good.

Step five: I release my word to the abundant and creative workings of Life. I let Life support me because it is always on my side. I let abundance be so in my world!

Treat Yourself to Love

Purpose of this treatment: To have a loving relationship. To love and be loved. To allow love to heal whatever feels unloved inside me; to let love within me heal others.

Step one: Life demonstrates its loving nature through creating. As Life breathes itself into all forms, it breathes love that heals and transforms. Love is in every good quality of Life. Beauty is love. Kindness is love. Peace is love. Love is the fundamental and natural energy of everything.

Step two: I can never be apart from Life; I can never be apart from love. It beats my heart. It gives me breath. One with Life, I know all of Life's wonderful qualities are within me. This love is within me now and always. It is the energy that draws people together and joins us.

Step three: I deserve love simply because I exist in an infinite field of love. I am willing to stop withholding love from others and from myself. Life loves everyone, and I choose love, too. I no longer believe I need a partner to feel whole, someone who proves to me I am lovable. Powered by love, my wholeness is established.

I allow the love that is already within me to fill me and to magnify beyond me. I have love to give and to share with others. As I radiate more and more love, I become a magnet for opportunities to share love. I experience love as a wellspring that never runs dry. I attract possibilities for the loving relationship I desire. A partner who is a perfect match for me is seeking me as I am seeking him/her. Together, we honor our wholeness, exactly as we are. Something wonderful and new is created by our combined loving energy.

Step four: I am thankful for this love I feel stirred up inside me. I am thankful for feeling love even now, knowing that as my new partner reveals himself/herself to me, more love is in store. I am grateful for all the ways in which the healing and creative vibration of love, by means of me, benefits others.

Step five: Life is bringing more love my way. I can feel it, and I expect it. My heart and eyes are wide open to the possibilities happening right now.

Treat Yourself to Peace and Happiness

Purpose of this treatment: To feel a general state of happiness, joy, contentment, and peace of mind. To respond calmly in all situations.

Step one: Life is orderly and harmonious. Everything and every person is an instrument in Life's beautiful symphony. Some people and situations are like harps and sweet flutes. Others are like brash trumpets or pounding timpani drums. Sometimes Life expresses itself as a soft lullaby, and sometimes Life expresses itself as a wild improvisation that seems without any other purpose than the sheer thrill of it.

Step two: Life's nature is my nature. Within me is a harmonious symphony. Life supports me and leads me in comfort and peace and joy. Because I am One with Life, all of its wonderful qualities are qualities within me.

Step three: No matter what happens around me, Life grounds me because it supports me and is on my side. No matter what calamity I see in the world, I know Life has greater power than any condition. Knowing Life is the source of everything, with every potential for healing and revealing more Life, I am never without hope and confidence that Life is in charge.

I accept my beautiful part to play in Life's various compositions. I express my aliveness into the world, and it brings me joy. Remembering I am a creative person with limitless possibilities fills me with contentment and happy anticipation. Life fills my sails with ideas and opportunities.

Every day I wake and choose joy. Every day I look for ways to share hope and peace. Every day I find places that need my certainty to lighten the hearts and minds of others. Every day I shine my light wherever there is darkness.

Step four: I am grateful to be alive. I am grateful to realize that Life is for me and for the world. I am grateful that hope is always stronger than desperation, that there is no limit to good and to Life's possibilities.

Step five: I accept my job to express Life and to represent Life. I expect Life to do its part by showing evidence of good in the midst of every situation. With this certainty, in partnership with Life, I am at peace.

Treat Yourself to Success

Purpose of this treatment: To shift my mindset to thoughts of success. To believe Life makes success possible for me. To expect success.

Step one: One Life creates and governs everything, every form of manifestation and experience. This Life orchestrates the cosmos, as well as the perfect rose blossoming in my garden. Life knows no limits of its expression and no boundaries of its power.

Step two: Life includes me and all of my activities. Its limitless creativity creates new possibilities though me. Its infinite intelligence informs everything I think and do. Its perfect law of manifestation stamps "successfully completed" on everything I put my attention to. It presents new ideas, opportunities, and partnerships that satisfy whatever is required for my success.

Step three: Life's intelligence inspires me with ideas and guides me in my activities. As I lift my thoughts to Life's higher vibration, I leave the world of problems, opinions, and market conditions.

With Life as my partner, nothing discourages me and everything leads me toward success.

I am a conduit for accomplishment, prosperity, abundance, and creativity. I welcome possibilities that require my receptivity to become something wonderfully new. This is where miracles exist, and this is where I live and breathe and think and create.

The never-before becomes possible when I believe it is. My experience is above average because I think above-average thoughts. Today, Life finds in me an opening for its greatest work, its inspired ideas, and its synchronicity of perfect action. Through me, Life accomplishes great things with ease.

Step four: I am grateful to be the voice, the hand, and the expression of Life's infinite possibilities. I am grateful for all the good in my life and all the good that is becoming by means of me. I am grateful to be Life's distributor of good by drawing others into this higher vibration of infinite abundance.

Step five: I release my word to the power of Life that responds to it. The higher vibration of my thoughts activates new possibilities and unleashes Life's perfect operation. Life goes before me, making my way easy, perfect, and successful. My success is assured.

Treat Yourself to Being Generous

Purpose of this treatment: To become more generous. To replicate Life's nature to give in my own life, keeping the flow of good going. I want to live to give.

Step one: Life's nature is to give unconditionally and constantly. It flows its qualities into the world in limitless abundance. In all things and through all people, there is an endless wellspring of good.

Step two: I am a wellspring of Life. Love flows through me. My creativity and specialness have no limits. Life is my distribution partner of good. I am a point of circulation to receive and share good.

Step three: I let go of any thoughts or beliefs about limitation, because Life is not limited and neither am I. I believe there is plenty of anything necessary for the expression of more Life.

I claim certainty in the infinite flow of good. I know good flows through me as easily as love appears within me whenever I require it.

Starting now, I act from a mindset of plenty. No matter what I have, there is enough to share, and more flows to me. I give because I receive so much. I give so that others may know Life supports them and is for them. I give so that I stand for a world that does have enough for everyone.

Starting now, I serve from a mindset of love. I am an emissary of love. I choose to serve as a powerful affirmation of my oneness with humanity. I find ways to serve throughout my day.

Step four: I am thankful to become one who lives to give and serve others. What more joyous way to spend Life than to share my good? I am grateful for being a conduit for Life's ever-expanding and loving nature.

Step five: I return my word to the source that inspired it. As I commit to partnering with Life, I know Life responds in kind. Opportunities to be generous are being manifested for me now.

Chapter 18

WHAT MATTERS NEXT?

THROUGHOUT THIS BOOK, YOU'VE been asked to be more and more willing. Where has the adventure of your willingness taken you? Has it invited you to see, believe, and expect something different, about Life and about yourself? Has willingness slowly unraveled what has bound you from feeling free and from being your true self? Has willingness broken down the walls of unworthiness to reveal your shining light that was there all along?

Willingness is deceiving. It appears subtle and charming, like the scent of a newborn baby or the softness of a puppy. Bit by bit, each point of willingness dissolves another layer of thoughts, beliefs, assumptions, habits, and patterns that have built up within you over the years. Willingness has the power to open the gates of your resistance and pry loose your grip on suffering.

Willingness has power because it is Life's power. Each time you allowed yourself to be willing, you allowed Life to reveal to you what has been true all along, true about Life and true about you. Willingness is Life's way of inviting you to see the better version of yourself, which is more powerful than all the layers of fear and suffering.

If you already experience a good life, maybe willingness has opened your mind and heart to new ways of growing your experience. As you become a conduit for good, you can help relieve suffering and maybe show others how to create something better.

There is actually no better version of you. You have always been an unrepeatable miracle. No matter what you've ever done or experienced, nothing has ever dimmed the light shining within you.

Let me share one last, and very powerful, story from my own life. I began this book with a story about my experience with my mother's Alzheimer's disease. Throughout my experience with her, I used the principles in this book. I did many Five Step Treatments to shift my mindset away from fear and separation and toward my partnership with Life. I was determined to see beyond the appearance of her disease so that Life's presence and activity could reveal something wonderful to me.

Eventually, it became clear she was nearing the end of her days. And yet she continued to live, without any awareness of her own and without any apparent quality to her life. With all of my certainty, I was challenged to find Life's presence in her seemingly empty state, lifeless in all ways except that her body was still functioning.

Why is she still alive? I wondered. As much as I tried, I couldn't understand how Life could be expressing through her. After all, I believe that if Life is present, there is potential and possibility. Existence confirms purpose: *If she is still here, there must be potential.* And then a new thought came to me: *Maybe the potential is for someone else. If my mother's existence makes something new possible, maybe this something new is not for her, or even for me, but for someone else.*

Miracles know no bounds. It's like water finding an outlet for its natural flow. With eyes wide open, I looked for evidence of Life's powerful and purposeful potential. *As long as she still breathes*, I believed, *she is a conduit for Life.* I expected it. Was she having an experience I couldn't see? Or was a new experience being created for someone else, something that required my mother, something Life might create by means of her and because of her?

And so one day my mother passed from this life. No one was with her; the nursing staff and family members were away from her room. Yet I still searched for evidence of Life's mysterious and miraculous ways.

I learned that the last person to be with my mother was my niece, her granddaughter. In the past, it had been too emotionally painful for my niece to witness her grandmother going through the unique changes that Alzheimer's brings. She saw her grandmother lose her beauty, her elegance, and her mental faculties entirely. It proved to be too much for her to bear.

Then, quite unexpectedly, she was drawn to begin visiting again. On her last visit, which was only hours before my mom's passing, she chose to read Maya Angelou's soothing words and also added loving words of her own. When I talked with her later, she told me it was one of the most deeply moving and loving experiences she ever had with her grandmother.

This was what I sought: proof that as long as we breathe, Life creates something new through us. My niece received a wonderful gift, a loving connection. It could have happened before, while her grandmother was still full of life, but it didn't. Nothing stops love. I choose to perceive this as perfect, right action and perfect, right timing. I choose to see a miracle. And I choose to believe that even after my mother's passing, this miracle and others since are still Life's mysterious way of creating something completely new, *because of* my mom's existence.

It is fitting that this is my last story, because it has great importance for all of us. We are here because Life requires us for its expression and expansion. We are here to be an inlet and an outlet of love and all things good. When we choose to be a willing and participating partner in this, we are able to allow more good to flow through us. More significantly, good can flow even when we're completely unaware of it. That is ultimately what we're here for. Through us, Life co-creates something better for us and for others. Because of us. Even more than we ever imagined. Miracles.

To me, this story reveals very important truths that have been discussed throughout this book.

We find what we seek. When we expect a miracle, we help make it possible. There are no limits to what's possible. Even if we're not aware. Even if we have no conscious awareness of ourselves and no recognition of our most beloved, Life still cherishes us and has use for us. As long as we breathe, there is potential, there is purpose. We matter.

Are you open to possibilities? Are you ready for a miracle?

The world waits for you to realize your gifts so that you may share them with us. Life waits for you to assume your partnership in expressing more Life that is only possible by you—because of you.

Imagine that this life is an amazing banquet. Everyone is invited. There's plenty for all. There are tables filled with more than you've ever dreamed. It's all available to you. Anything you choose will be deliciously satisfying. So, what will you choose when everything is so very good?

In your life right now, Life offers every kind of good, everything that will bring you joy and fulfillment. It doesn't matter what you do next, nor what you choose next. What matters is that you realize that *you* matter. Because you are here, you matter. Because you matter, Life will provide everything you require to live your best life, your way.

What you desire not only will make you happy but will make the world happy. In a connected world, where there is only One Life, anyone's happiness contributes to everyone's happiness.

Think Better. Live Better.

Because better for one is better for all.

ACKNOWLEDGMENTS

IT TAKES MORE THAN A VILLAGE. It takes a lifetime to develop thoughts that become published. It also takes saying yes when an idea grabs you and won't let go. It's virtually impossible to acknowledge everyone who has helped make this book possible. So, as most authors do, I will give thanks to those who had the most direct involvement in what you've just read.

Above all, Dr. Ernest Holmes provided the greatest gift to me and to millions when he developed a powerful technique called Spiritual Mind Treatment, which is taught in this book as the Five Step Treatment. I choose to believe he'd be pleased with my own thoughts that I've contributed to it.

My gratitude knows no bounds for the priceless wisdom I receive from my mentor, partner, and dear friend Rev. Dr. Lloyd George Tupper. May we share many more moments and years of abundant living.

Those who teach and inspire me are too numerous to mention, but I want to give special mention to a few: Dr. Michael Beckwith,

Dr. Wayne Dyer, Rev. Karyl Huntley, Posi Lyon, Janet Carol Ryan, Michael Hart, and my loving friends of Golden Gate Center For Spiritual Living.

Thank you to dear friends and family who helped this book become something better: Lilly Collis, Bill Russell, Ken Schmidt, Charlene Keller, Gail Durkin, Jane Paxton Hoffman, Rick Walt, Linda Mason, Lori Greer, Ann Amtower, Sue Rouda (and again to Posi, Janet, Karyl, Phil, and Lloyd).

Thanks to my publisher, Brooke Warner of She Writes Press, and her supportive and experienced goddesses of "partnership publishing." Know that many lives are changing, positively and permanently, by means of all of you and because of you.

I'll acknowledge my husband, Phil, once again for his many readings, genius thoughts, creative collaboration, loving patience, and infinite faith. And, of course, I honor my dear mom, who gave her greatest gifts to me in moments she never knew. Through you, mom, Life continues to present opportunities for my own transformation and inspiration for others.

Above all, my cup runneth over with love for all the ways Life lives through me, inviting me to live better and dream bigger every day. I am thankful that I don't believe in writer's block. And I am grateful to you, dear reader, for letting Life stir something new in you, whether by timid willingness or by amazing revelation. Let us all create a better life and a better world.

ABOUT THE AUTHOR

FRANCINE HUSS is an author, speaker, teacher, and consultant.

Francine is passionate about helping people discover their significance, realize their potential, and create their best life. She's also passionate about helping the business world create better lives, better business and a better world. Visit her website for more about her professional experience that qualifies Francine as an expert in creativity.

Francine and her husband live in Healdsburg, California and Lake Michigan, where their lemon-pie dream life includes dogs, vineyards, sunsets, travel, music, craft beer, entertaining family and friends, creating original art, designing beautiful spaces, and living spiritual abundance.

FOR YOUR GROUP OR ORGANIZATION

IMAGINE SHARING THE IDEAS and techniques in *Think Better. LIVE BETTER.* with others. Introduce your employees, students, and like-minded groups to these simple yet powerful principles. Make a choice to help create the world you wish for.

Contact us for:
Volume discounts on books
Group-discussion outlines
Book-study programs
Workbook sales

Francine Huss is available for consulting, executive coaching, employee creativity and motivational programs, and leadership workshops.

Special Offer
"Better" just keeps getting better. Download a free gift with new ideas on jump-starting your better life today. Visit www.francinehuss.com for details.

www.ingramcontent.com/pod-product-compliance
Lightning Source LLC
Chambersburg PA
CBHW021502170125
20462CB00004B/174

* 9 7 8 1 9 3 8 3 1 4 6 6 7 *